CANALS *of* ENGLAND

CANALS *of* ENGLAND

Text by Martin Marix Evans
Photographs Robert Reichenfeld

Weidenfeld and Nicolson
London

Text © Martin Marix Evans
Photographs © Robert Reichenfeld

The right of Martin Marix Evans and Robert Reichenfeld to be identified as authors of this work
has been asserted by them in accordance with the Copyright, Designs and Patents Act 1988.

First published in Great Britain in 1994 by
George Weidenfeld and Nicolson Ltd
The Orion Publishing Group
Orion House
5 Upper St Martin's Lane
London WC2H 9EA

Designed by Paul Ryan
Map by Baz East
Printed and bound in Italy

British Library Cataloguing-in-Publication Data
A catalogue record for this book is available from the British Library.

ISBN 297 83261 1

In association with

British Waterways

British Waterways, which runs the country's network of canals and rivers, are celebrating 200 years of canals with
a series of public events and festivals. To find out more about Canals 200, please contact:
British Waterways, Customer Services, Willow Grange, Church Road, Watford WD1 3QA

Half-title page: Northampton. By way of an arm at Gayton, the Grand
Union, which brings together all of England's essetial waterways,
joins the Nene Navigation and thus access to the sea.

Page 2: Summit, Greater Manchester. Jessop's audacious Rochdale
Canal crosses the Pennine watershed.

Title page: Market Drayton, Shropshire. The aggressive
direct line of the Shropshire Union is typical of Telford's approach.

CONTENTS

INTRODUCTION

The passage of two centuries has softened the impact of canals upon the landscape of Britain. Where once the raw materials and manufactured goods of the
Industrial Revolution weighed down the slow-moving boats, most cargoes
today are pleasure-seeking holiday makers. The waterways that wind through
the fields or climb the steep hill are now quiet.

Before the eighteenth century travel was by road or by river. The legacy of
the Romans, straight, well-paved highways, decayed, having been designed to
serve the needs of a military regime more than a thousand years earlier. People
moved on foot, on horseback and by coach, cart and wagon. In wet weather the
surface was quickly reduced to rutted mud. To move heavy loads over the hills
on winding tracks by cart or wagon was virtually impossible, and pack-horses
were used. Carriage by water, in coasters or in barges on the rivers, was used
where possible.

Natural rivers, however, are limited in their usefulness for transportation.
The waters rise and fall according to the vagaries of the weather, millers construct weirs to create heads of water to drive their machinery, farmers extract
water to irrigate their crops: all these activities obstruct the voyager. To
improve the rivers Acts of Parliament were needed to authorize 'navigations'
and to override the resistance of the vested interests in their previous use. From
the sixteenth century onwards there were numerous acts to improve or restore
rivers throughout the kingdom, providing the only practical means to transport
heavy loads.

The trading pattern of Britain thus depended on boats. Sea-coal came to
London from Newcastle, China clay from Cornwall to the Mersey and then
inefficiently on to Stoke. Where a town or region had access to a navigable
river, trade could prosper, but for the greater part industry and business were

local affairs, based in villages and dependent on market towns for sales. In the 1720s Daniel Defoe stated the problem in terms of a staple food, cheese: 'Warwickshire men have no water-carriage at all, or at least not 'till they have carry'd it a long way by land to Oxford . . . Land-carriage being long, and the ways bad, makes it very dear to the poor, who are the consumers.'

This situation could not persist; new pressures demanded change. The invention of new machines was transforming the manufacture of goods, concentrating the centres of production and population. Economic bulk transport had to follow.

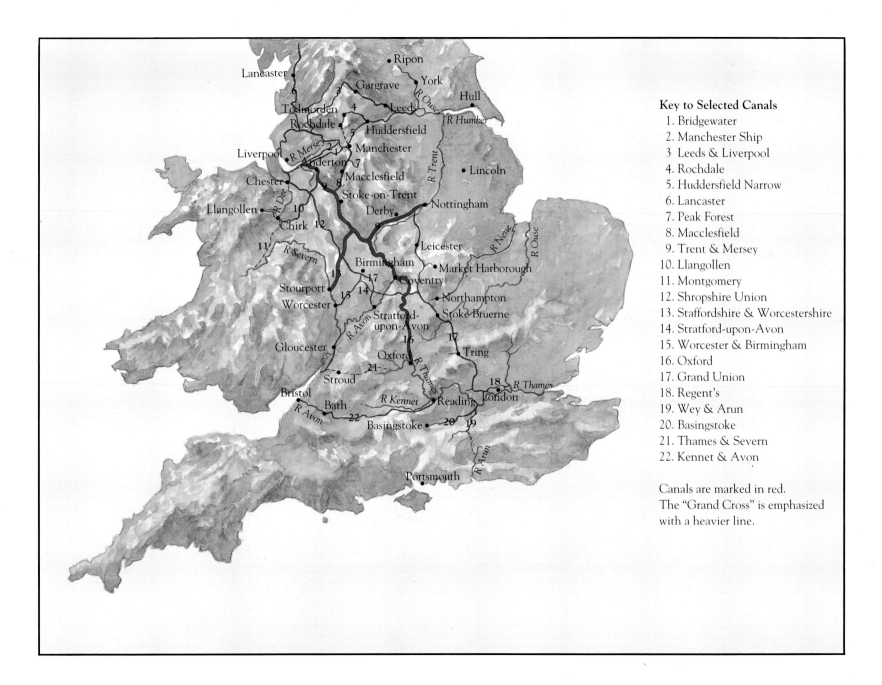

Key to Selected Canals

1. Bridgewater
2. Manchester Ship
3. Leeds & Liverpool
4. Rochdale
5. Huddersfield Narrow
6. Lancaster
7. Peak Forest
8. Macclesfield
9. Trent & Mersey
10. Llangollen
11. Montgomery
12. Shropshire Union
13. Staffordshire & Worcestershire
14. Stratford-upon-Avon
15. Worcester & Birmingham
16. Oxford
17. Grand Union
18. Regent's
19. Wey & Arun
20. Basingstoke
21. Thames & Severn
22. Kennet & Avon

Canals are marked in red.
The "Grand Cross" is emphasized
with a heavier line.

THE BIRTHPLACE OF THE CANAL: THE NORTH

Barton
Greater Manchester

In 1893 a new waterway cut
through Brindley's Bridgewater
canal, and sea-going ships could
sail into Manchester itself.
Today a slender viaduct lifts the
M6 motorway, a yet newer artery
of commerce, over the
Manchester Ship Canal.

Dominating the northern landscape are the Pennine hills, which run from the Scottish border almost to the centre of England. Their upper slopes of limestone and millstone grit create a beautifully harsh country of moorland and peat bog, and on their flanks, in Lancashire and southern Yorkshire, are the coal-bearing rocks that were to provide the power base of the region's great industries. Initially power came from water, and the valley slopes were dotted with small manufactories in which a family might be found spinning or weaving. The towns were centres of distribution as much as production, and the small scale of operations meant that transportation was a problem that could, though not without difficulty, be overcome.

To the west of the Pennines a few short rivers run down to the sea, while the broader lowlands to the east are served with a more complex system draining into the Humber – the Yorkshire Ouse, the Aire, the Calder, and, curving up from the south, the Trent. One of the last great river navigations, the Calder and Hebble, which gave Halifax access to the sea, was completed by John Smeaton by authority of the Acts of Parliament passed in 1758 and 1769. The inland port of Goole was a creation of the great riverway system in the east, reaching as far north as York and Ripon, but goods still moved to and from Lancashire by pack-horse over the daunting hills.

Had the beautiful Elizabeth Gunning looked more kindly on the love of young Francis Egerton, 3rd Duke of Bridgewater, the canal age might have started somewhere else. But she did not. So Bridgewater turned his back on London and returned to his estates, which included the coal mines at Worsley. Here he found two major problems. The workings were filling with water, and in the days before efficient steam-driven pumps a scheme to drain the mines was essential if they were not to be abandoned. Secondly, the coal itself had to be transported by cart or pack-horse to the nearest market of size, Manchester. Though only some ten miles away, the carriage costs doubled the price to the customer.

Bridgewater's father had considered the transport problem, and obtained an act in 1737 to turn Worsley brook into a navigation, a plan that was never realized. Like so many wealthy young men of the age, Francis Egerton had made the Grand Tour, seen the

Canal du Midi in France, and was aware of the possibilities. At the same time, he had as his agent one John Gilbert, whose brother Thomas was agent to the Earl of Gower, the employer of James Brindley. Originally a millwright, Brindley was a self-educated man, and a genius. In 1752 he had been employed to drain Wet Earth colliery, Clifton, on the river Irwell, and for Gower and Josiah Wedgwood he had surveyed the proposed canal to join the Trent to the Mersey. Brindley joined the new undertaking in July 1759, after Bridgewater had obtained an act 'to make a navigable Cut or Canal from a certain place in the township of Salford, to or near Worsley Mill and Middlewood in the manor of Worsley'.

The original scheme was to bring the canal down to the River Irwell by locks, and up again on the other side by locks. Brindley favoured as few locks as possible to save time and water. After what he described in his diary as an 'ochilor servey or ricconitoring', he proposed what was seen as impossible: an aqueduct at Barton, lofting the canal over the river. After objections to the aqueduct had been overcome, it is said, by a demonstration model constructed by Brindley from cheese, the necessary powers were obtained from parliament in 1760. Thus, following the natural contour of the land, the connection could be made with a ten-and-a-half-mile canal entirely on one level. This involved building embankments, which the critics claimed would never hold water, but Brindley solved the problem with clay puddling – clay worked up with water and trodden down as a lining to the earthworks, a pioneering device that would be used everywhere thereafter.

At Worsley the canal ran underground, right into the mines, drawing from them the water supply required and draining the mines at the same time. Boats, known as 'starvationers' because of their exposed ribs, were loaded underground, but again Brindley enhanced the process with an innovation. At both ends of the canal there were problems with handling the coal. The mines operated on various different levels, and at the final destination, Salford, the canal ended at the foot of a hill. By loading the coal into containers and placing them in the boats, and by building a short tunnel at Salford and a shaft to the surface at the top of the hill, the goods could be winched into and out of the vessels just where required.

The impact of the completed canal was immense. The price of coal in Manchester halved to 4d. per hundredweight. Sightseers were amazed though sometimes critical of the raw gash through the countryside and compared the man-made creation unfavourably to the natural beauty of the river. Above all, businessmen were impressed, for it was clearly profitable. In the *Manchester Mercury* , 'C. S.' reported in 1763 on 'the Duke of Bridgewater's Navigation':

> His projector, the ingenious Mr Brindley, has indeed made such improvements in this way as are truly astonishing. At Barton bridge, he has erected a navigable canal in the air; for it is as high as the tops of the trees. Whilst I was surveying it with a mixture of wonder and delight, four barges passed me in the space of about three minutes, two of them being chained together, and dragged by two horses, who went on the terras of the canal, whereon, I must own, I durst hardly venture to walk, as I trembled to behold the River Irwell beneath me.

By 1763 the canal had been extended to Manchester, and the development to the west to join the Mersey was approved. In 1766 Wedgwood and his colleagues got their act for the Trent to Mersey connection, and a deal was done with Bridgewater to change his line to link the two. Manchester now had a reliable outlet to the sea, and a strong trade grew that brought in raw cotton from the seaport and coal from the mines, as well as being able to ship finished cotton goods out to world markets, which enriched the canal owners in the process. A century later an even larger undertaking, the Manchester Ship Canal, would require the destruction of Brindley's trail-blazing aqueduct, to be replaced by the remarkable swing aqueduct that is there today.

The Bridgewater was a broad canal, designed to accommodate the local river craft, 'Mersey flats' as they were called, and locks at the western end of the system were made fourteen feet wide. The approach Brindley took – keeping as closely as possible to a single level – meant that the water supply was not critical in this case. Major cross-country canals, however, were a different matter. In the high hills a constant supply of water was harder to find, and narrow canals were necessary. When planning his next great work, the Trent and Mersey canal, Brindley decided to build his locks seven feet wide and 72 feet long; hence the maximum dimensions of the narrow boat.

Josiah Wedgwood had long been aware of the advantages canal transport could bring to his pottery business. The raw material he required came from Cornwall or Devon by ship to the Mersey, then was loaded into barges to travel south up the Weaver and completed its journey by pack-horse. The finished product also went out by pack-horse, and he allowed for some two-thirds of all he despatched to get broken on the way. To link the Mersey with the Trent at Burton-on-Trent would give safe, water-borne access to east and west, and a further link to the Severn to the south would shorten and cheapen supply lines. The line would pass through the great salt-producing area of Cheshire, offering similar advantages to businessmen there.

Brindley faced new challenges in linking Stoke-on-Trent to the Mersey. Between Middlewich and his target he needed 31 locks, and altogether the canal was to extend to 140 miles with 160 aqueducts of varying sizes, 109 road bridges, 75 locks and five tunnels, including the Harecastle tunnel. At the top of the climb to the south, before dropping down to Stoke, the Harecastle had to be over a mile and a half long and, like his aqueduct at Barton, many said it would be impossible to build.

In Lives of the Engineers Samuel Smiles writes:

> Shafts were sunk from the hill-top at different points down to the level of the intended canal. The stuff was drawn out of the shafts in the usual way by horse-gins; and so long as the water was met with in but small quantities, the power of windmills and watermills working pumps over each shaft was sufficient to keep the excavators at work. But as the miners descended and cut through the various strata of the hill on their downwards progress water was met with in vast quantities; and here Brindley's skill in pumping machinery proved of great value . . . This abundance of water, though it was a serious hindrance to the execution of the work, was a circumstance on which Brindley had calculated, and indeed, depended, for the supply of water for the summit level of his canal.

The work was completed and the canal opened in 1777, but the great engineer was not there to see it. James Brindley died in 1772.

Further north, the great barrier of the Pennines remained unconquered. Plans had been made, and an Act of Parliament obtained, for the construction of the Leeds and Liverpool broad canal to connect the great industrial areas of Yorkshire and Lancashire early enough for Brindley to be involved in surveying the line, and work started in 1770. On the Yorkshire side the situation was quite clear: from Leeds the Aire and Calder gives access to the Humber and the North Sea, and an obvious line runs in the opposite direction, the north-west, up Airedale to Skipton and Gargrave. Not that it was an easy route to follow – there are 29 locks in 29 miles. Eight of these are concentrated in the Bingley

Five- and Three-Rise. A rise is a staircase lock in which the upper gates of one chamber form the lower gates of the next. The arrangement is not the most efficient, as boats cannot pass one another in the lock and a great deal of water is used, but the gain in height can be dramatic. The Bingley Five-Rise has a lift of 59 feet. By 1777 this length was complete and starting to earn its keep.

On the Lancashire side things did not proceed so smoothly. There was much argument about the line to be followed, and when that was settled the War of American Independence intervened, money ran short, and still the high Pennine watershed had to be overcome. Work ceased, but the two ends of the system were in service and making enough money to pay investors a modest dividend.

A rival to the Leeds and Liverpool route had been proposed as early as 1766, when a group of Rochdale businessmen asked Brindley to survey a trans-Pennine link with the Calder and Hebble canal at Halifax. With the cessation of hostilities with America and the growing realization that canals were good investments, the scheme was revived. New surveys were undertaken by John Rennie and William Crossley, Sr, for a narrow canal, like the one favoured by Brindley for crossing difficult country. Fortunately, the attempt to get an act for this scheme in 1793 failed, and William Jessop was consulted. He proposed a further series of seven locks to lift a broad canal clean across the hills, and in 1794 the necessary act was passed for a 33-mile canal with 92 locks. This new plan gained the agreement of Bridgewater, despite a substantial toll on all goods, other than flagstones, carried from Rochdale, but a rare continuity of facilities had been achieved. Incoherent development of canals by numerous private undertakings was to be a lasting disadvantage to waterway transport.

Work began at once, and by 1799 the two ends of the canal were complete. Again the cost was higher than forecast, and progress was delayed. The final flights of locks to the summit were not finished at Todmorden and Littleborough until 1804. Finally the first canal across the Pennines was complete. Samuel Smiles writes:

> From the rugged nature of the country over which the canal had to be carried – having to be lifted from lock to lock over the great mountain-ridge known as 'the backbone of England' – few works have had greater physical obstacles to encounter . . . In crossing the range at one place, a stupendous cutting, fifty feet deep, had to be blasted through hard

rock. In other places, where it climbs along the face of a hill, it is overhung by precipices. On the Yorkshire side, at Todmorden, the valley grows narrower and narrower, overhung by steep, almost perpendicular, rocks of millstone-grit, with room, in many parts, for only the waterway, the turnpike road, and the little river Calder in the bottom of the ravine.

The 1790s were the years of canal mania. Throughout the kingdom schemes were hatched, meetings held, and investors thrust their money at all manner of undertakings from the scatter-brained to the astute. Industry's hunger for raw materials – coal, iron ore, limestone, china clay – the need to send out their products and to supply the inhabitants of the growing towns offered the prospect of vast toll revenues. Qualified engineers were few, tended to accept too many commissions and were tempted to delegate jobs to incapable people.

The proprietors of the Ashton canal, connecting Manchester with towns immediately to the east and south, struggled until joined by Benjamin Outram in 1798. Cooperative links with other canals conflicted with rivalry for routes. Ashton beat the Rochdale to building a branch to Hollinwood but needed a connection with the Rochdale to gain an outlet to the west. Such links allowed the existing canal's owners to drive hard bargains on shares of tolls and access to water. In the face of these problems, the Ashton owners supported a scheme by others that they had originally planned to undertake themselves, the Peak Forest canal, for which an act was obtained in 1794.

The plan was originally to build the canal via Marple to Chapel Milton and lay a tramway to the limestone quarries at Dove Holes, between Chapel-en-le-Frith and Buxton. Later, it was decided to stop at Bugsworth (now gentrified to 'Buxworth') and to extend the tramway from there to Chapel Milton higher up the valley. Outram had experience in building tramways and was appointed engineer to the project. Forerunners to the railways, tramways allowed wagons to run on iron tracks of L-shaped section, the vertical member being set to the inside edge to guide the unflanged wheels, and the wagons were drawn by horses. The tramways were a practical solution in difficult country, but limited in the size of load they could handle.

Running north-east from the junction of the Ashton and Peak Forest canals is the most audacious of the trans-Pennine waterways, the Huddersfield Narrow canal. Just as the Rochdale took a more direct route than the Leeds and Liverpool, so this venture relied on a route over the high moors, almost a direct line from Manchester to Huddersfield. From there boats could use the broad canal to join the Calder and Hebble. But the necessity of building narrow passageways, saving water and making tunnelling practicable led to the recurring problem of compatability. Locks on the Calder and Hebble were built to suit Yorkshire keels, only 58 feet in length, while the narrow canal was built to the Midland gauge of 70 feet by seven feet. Without transferring loads, therefore, use was limited to short and less economical boats. Nonetheless, the Huddersfield Narrow boasts England's highest and longest canal tunnel, beneath Standedge. Over three miles in length, it is nearly 650 feet above sea level, and the hills rise above it by a further 600 feet, making it the deepest tunnel as well. It caused Outram considerable difficulties and took twelve years to drill.

Like so many of the canals of Britain, the Huddersfield Narrow was abandoned in the face of competition, first from the railways and then from the roads, but is now in the course of restoration. Possibly the last person to navigate Standedge tunnel before it closed was L. T. C. Rolt in the days of steam railways. He describes the experience in *The Inland Waterways of England* (1950):

> The tunnel is not brick-lined throughout, nor is it of uniform size. On the contrary, for the greater part of its length the walls and roof are of jagged rock which reveals to this day the shot holes of those intrepid 'navigators' who blasted their way through the Pennines a century and a half ago. In places these rock walls recede and for a short space the narrow cave becomes a roomy cavern where boats were able to pass each other . . . There are ventilation shafts at intervals, but these contribute only the faintest glimmer of light to the depths, for the shafts are anything up to 600 ft. deep, while their mouths are protected by stout timber stagings to guard against rock falls. Upon each side at a slightly higher level run the railway tunnels, for the railway engineers made use of the canal tunnel for construction work, drainage and ventilation. At the passage of an express the rocks reverberate with a dull thunder of sound and a sudden blast of air is soon followed by a blinding cloud of acrid smoke which bellies out from the cross galleries. Altogether a closer approximation of the legendary route to the infernal regions by way of the Styx it would be difficult to conceive.

Worsley
Greater Manchester

James Brindley, a 43-year-old self-educated millwright, was charged with two tasks at Worsley: the drainage of the coal mines and the construction of a canal to carry the coals to Manchester. He designed the Bridgewater Canal to run into the mines themselves, providing the required drainage and simplifying the handling of the coal. The entrances are now barred for security, though water still drains from them, stained with iron ore, which is present in small quantities. There are 46 miles of underground canals on two levels beyond this arch. Using a sluice gate, the water level inside the mine was allowed to rise while boats were being loaded with tubs of coal. Then, raising the sluice, a flow was created to flush the laden boats into the canal, ready to be towed to Manchester.

Worsley
Greater Manchester

The half-timbered façade of the Packet House overlooks the canal basin at Worsley Delph. The canals were not used solely for the transportation of goods and raw materials. Swift packet boats competed with stagecoaches, and this is where a regular luxury passenger service to Castlefield in Manchester started its journey. To travel at the front of the boat was preferable; two shillings was the fare for the 'front room' and one shilling for the 'back room'. A traveller on the Lancaster Canal reported in 1839 that it was 'the most delightful journey I ever made in my life . . . The manner in which we went along the way was for beauty of motion unequalled'. The Bridgewater packet boats last ran in 1872.

Barton
Greater Manchester

Brindley's Bridgewater Canal from Worsley to Manchester had to cross the River Irwell. The obvious solution was to come down to the river level by locks and by lock up again on the other side, but this would delay the passage of the boats. His solution, revolutionary for the time, was to build an aqueduct to carry the canal above the river and to keep it on a level. The structure was massive, built to support not only the weight of water but also the earthworks to hold it. The sides and bed of the waterway were of earth and puddled clay, just like the channel dug on land. When the Manchester Ship Canal was constructed, the Irwell was absorbed into it and the Barton Swing Aqueduct was devised by Edward Leader Williams to give access to sea-going vessels while allowing the continuing use of the Bridgewater. Built in 1893, it spans 235 feet and weighs 1450 tons. In spite of its size, the structure possesses a simple beauty. The remains of the original stone aqueduct can be seen at either end.

**Sowerby Bridge
West Yorkshire**

The honest face of this ware-house provides access to boats to load cargo under cover. The Rochdale was the first trans-Pennine waterway to be completed, and from 1804 it carried the bulk of the business between Yorkshire and Lancashire. It joins the Calder and Hebble navigation at this point and thus connects by river navigations to the Humber. The impact of the river navigations on trade was commented on by Daniel Defoe, who observed of the Aire and Calder Navigation: 'A communication by water was opened from Leeds and Wakefield to Hull, and by which means all the woolen manufactures which those merchants now export . . . is carried by water to Hull, and there shipped for Holland, Bremen, Hamburgh, and the Baltick.'

Sowerby Bridge
West Yorkshire

Beneath the steep walls of
Calderdale a broad boat with
a stout mast lies moored at
Sowerby Bridge basin, a bicycle
chained to its winch. Sail was
rarely used on the canals, but
masts were used to keep tow-
ropes aloft; in the open country
crossed by the rivers of east
Yorkshire sail was practical. The
Rochdale was built broad, and
the boats built for the canal
were also broad.

Sowerby Bridge
West Yorkshire

An impression of ease is given by a boat moored on the Rochdale Canal, sheltered by the wooded banks of Calderdale. The moors above are harsh and weather-beaten, and in the depths of winter this pleasant scene is transformed by snow and ice. The competition of the railways and, later, roads ruined the canal business. But in recent years a growing appreciation of the leisure opportunities that they afford and the devotion of restoration societies have revived it. Locks have been brought back into working order, wharves and buildings refurbished, and even the signposts replaced in proper form.

Sowerby Bridge
West Yorkshire

As it climbs eastwards from
Sowerby Bridge and Halifax, the
Rochdale Canal competes for
space with the River Calder and
the roads, not to mention farmland. It was often necessary to
blast a ledge on the rockface,
using hand drills to make the
shot-holes, to hold the waterway
and to build bridges for roads
crossing the canal or to support
overhanging rocks. The scars of
construction have long healed,
and the canal-side rock face provides a precarious hold for spring
flowers. The cuts made in the
bridge abutments by grit-encrust-
ed tow-ropes also endure.

**Hebden Bridge
West Yorkshire**

Roads, railway, river and canal cram together as they climb towards the Pennine watershed from Hebden Bridge. As Samuel Smiles observed, 'the valley grows narrower and narrower, overhung by steep, almost perpendicular, rocks of millstone-grit, with room, in many parts, for only the waterway, the turnpike road and the little river Calder in the bottom of the ravine'. The bare moorland contrasts with the tree-covered slopes below. Down in the dale the canal is at left, and moving to the right are the narrow river, the main road, the railway and a minor road.

**Hebden Bridge
West Yorkshire**

Hebden Bridge shows its industrial past clearly and proudly. The mills of Hebden were and still are famous for their corduroy. The town lies in a constricted triangle alongside the Calder, and the hills covered with small houses built for the workers rise steeply behind it. On the open moors above, some mills still stand, though they have been abandoned and turned over to recreational use or divided up into small commercial units. An old pack-horse road winds up through a 'clough' – a little side valley – towards Pecket Well and passes a dye-works still in production on the way to a mill standing high above the valley. By such roads the manufactured goods were brought down to the canal for shipment. Before the canal came, the pack-horse was the only means by which goods could be taken down to Sowerby Bridge or west to Lancashire.

**Gauxholme
West Yorkshire**

The railway, the eventual conqueror of the canals, crosses the Rochdale by a grandiloquent castellated bridge at the foot of the final 17-lock flight from Todmorden to the summit. As the valley narrows, canal and road vie for the space, and the railway, as the lastcomer, is forced to use what is left. Local materials were used by the builders of all three transport systems, giving a harmony to works undertaken many decades apart.

**Todmorden
West Yorkshire**

The 18th-century road bridge at Todmorden is all in stone, while its more recent cousin makes extensive use of iron. In spring this is a misleadingly attractive scene. The sheltered canal is liable to freezing over in winter, and ice-breaking boats were needed to keep the way open for commercial traffic.

**Todmorden
West Yorkshire**

The barrenness of the wind-
swept moors contrasts with the
wooded valleys, as the Rochdale
Canal climbs out of Calderdale.
In the 1720s Daniel Defoe trav-
elled the more direct route from
Rochdale to Halifax over
Blackstone Edge to the east.
Although it was July, he wrote
that snow covered the ground
and that a blizzard put his party
in danger of their lives, 'and a
poor spaniel dog that was my fel-
low traveller . . . turn'd tail to it
and cry'd'.

**Steanor Bottom
West Yorkshire**

The turnpike toll-house near
Todmorden. Defoe, a vociferous
critic of the roads' condition,
advocated turnpikes as a solution
to the problems of travel. The
financial burden of maintaining
the roads in his time fell on the
owners of the land over which
the thoroughfare passed, which
produced predictable results:
repairs were few and skimped.
The introduction of turnpikes –
roads charging a toll to travellers
– made funds available, in theo-
ry, to keep them in good condition. For passenger traffic it was
helpful, but heavy goods made
excessive demands on the surface. In fact, until the coming of
the railways, canals were the
sinews of economic growth.

**Todmorden
West Yorkshire**

Close to the tree-line, the
Rochdale approaches the summit. The construction and materials of a barn are echoed in the
canal bridge below.

**Todmorden
West Yorkshire**

Above the lock entrance a foot-
bridge of a design characteristic
of, though not unique to, the
Rochdale canal. Arrangements
and lock gear vary from one part
of England to another, sometimes because of local needs or
available materials, or simply
because the engineer responsible
decided he had a better way of
doing things.

Summit
Greater Manchester

Concealed by stone walls typical
of the hill country, the canal
starts down from Summit lock,
its presence revealed only by the
boats' upperworks.

Summit
Greater Manchester

The final lock of the flight up
from Todmorden is marked by
the white lock-keeper's cottage,
with the moors towering high
above. As Samuel Smiles
remarks, 'Few works have had
greater physical obstacles to
encounter than this between
Rochdale and Todmorden.'

Marsden
West Yorkshire

Now closed to traffic, though it is hoped eventually to be restored, the entrance to the Standedge Tunnel is barred. At Marsden, the Huddersfield Narrow Canal is nearly 650 feet above sea level, the highest canal in the land. On emerging from the tunnel, after travelling over 3 miles through the gloom and marking their progress by the numbered plaques on the walls at 50-yard intervals, boatmen would see the fields above Marsden with hills towering another 600 feet above. The tunnel itself is lined with brick at its opening but runs largely through the raw rock of the Pennines. It is irregular in size, presumably because the rock was cut and blasted back until stability was achieved. In places it is only eight and a half feet high, and the channel is seven and a half feet wide, except where, according to Rolt, 'these rock walls recede and for a short space the narrow cave becomes a roomy cavern where boats were able to pass each other'.

Anderton
Cheshire

The mighty Anderton lift, built in 1875, provided the vital water connection between the River Weaver navigation, which ran north to the Mersey, and the Trent and Mersey canal to Stoke and the Potteries, cutting out the round-about route by the Bridgewater. The lift was capable of taking two narrow boats in each of its two caissons, great iron tubs 75 feet long and 15 and a half feet wide. These containers were arranged to counterbalance one another, and a steam engine provided the power to operate the hydraulic rams of the lift. It strains credulity to descend such a lift in a little pleasure boat, which seems to counterbalance two fully loaded boats coming up in the other caisson. Early in the 20th century, electricity replaced steam, and the caissons were converted to independent operation using counterbalance weights. The Anderton lift is seen here in the course of restoration, probably closer to its original appearance than in its later years of use.

Anderton
Cheshire

The River Weaver drains into the Mersey and forms part of the system by which raw materials were brought to Cheshire and Staffordshire before the days of the canals. The river was made into a navigation in the 1720s. The kaolin used for Wedgwood pottery came from Cornwall to the Mersey and up the Weaver before being carried by pack horse on to Stoke. The finished goods made the return journey the same way, with considerable breakage. The salt extraction industry of Cheshire also made use of this waterway, but again overland carriage was a significant and expensive link in the transportation. The Weaver is able to accommodate large boats, and the substantial locks make use of a simple but effective signalling system similar to that of the railway.

Anderton
Cheshire

Brick ventilation shafts, using those originally employed to extract the spoil of the diggings, serve the Preston Brook Tunnel, 1239 yards of darkness beneath the meadows. It was impossible to find a route for the Trent and Mersey on a single level, as Brindley had done for the Bridgewater. Two major tunnels and 75 locks were needed. The longest tunnel was the 2880-yard Harecastle Tunnel at the summit north of Stoke, the fame of which has eclipsed the achievement in the building of the Preston Brook Tunnel.

Anderton
Cheshire

A white-painted bridge, typical of the Trent and Mersey, shows up well by night to assist navigation. It was more usual to outline only the arch of the bridge in white or to use a pale stone. Boats worked long hours, starting before dawn and pushing on as long as possible into the night, provided the business was available. The majority of the boats were owned by the great transport companies, such as Pickfords and Fellows, Morton and Clayton. Others were the property of 'Number Ones' – owner-boatmen, who got cargoes subcontracted by the major carriers. Pay was based on the tonnage carried, an incentive to work long and hard when business was plentiful but a precarious source of income in hard times.

Anderton
Cheshire

Josiah Wedgwood and the salt merchants of Cheshire teamed up to promote a canal to serve not only their needs for a connection with the Mersey but to give them access to the Humber by way of the Trent at Shardlow. Brindley was engaged to undertake the work, and a line from the Trent ran 92 miles to Preston Brook, near Runcorn, where it joined the Bridgewater Canal and thus led to both Manchester and the sea. Taking the Bridgewater into the route to the Mersey had the advantage of giving the duke an interest in supporting the proposal against the resistance of the owners of the river navigations, who feared to lose by the new scheme. The Trent and Mersey was to form the first two arms of Brindley's 'Grand Cross' of canals. The journey from the potteries to the Mersey was longer than it had been by way of the Weaver. But the goods were shipped in bulk by narrow boats without further handling on the way, and breakages ceased to be a problem.

Marple
Greater Manchester

A threatening evening storm appears over the Peak Forest canal. To the east of Manchester, the Ashton canal connects the city with the Huddersfield Narrow Canal and with the Peak Forest, which pushes up into the hills to the south. The canal was a combination of waterway and plate tramway, built by Benjamin Outram, who demonstrated the ability of the late-18th-century engineers to overcome obstacles considered insurmountable a couple of decades earlier. The line ran up to Marple, with its superb acqueduct, and on to Whaley Bridge, where it connected with the Cromford and High Peak Railway leading to the Cromford canal and eventually Nottingham. A branch ran to Bugsworth Basin, where the plate railway completed the line up to the limestone quarries at Dove Holes.

Marple
Greater Manchester

A rare exception to the use of stone on the Peak Forest Canal – Brick Bridge No. 19. The curving path from the waterside is characteristic of a 'turnover', or rove, bridge. From place to place the lie of the land forces the towpath from one side of the canal to the other, so the towing horse must cross. A turnover bridge allows the horse to pass beneath, plod up the curved ramp, over the bridge, and down the straight ramp on the other side without casting off the tow-rope.

Marple
Greater Manchester

Telford's Macclesfield Canal cuts a corner on the route from Manchester to the Midlands by leaving the Peak Forest at Marple and striking off direct for the Trent and Mersey some six miles north of Stoke. No. 1 Bridge at the junction with the Peak Forest is a beautiful turnover bridge, partly concealed in this view by the warehouse or mill house, which has a dock under cover for boats or carts to load and unload alongside. The seatings for the old stop-lock can be seen in the stonework alongside the building where the canal narrows. By closing a stop-lock, water could be prevented from flowing from one canal to another, should the level of one of them drop, thereby endangering the water supply of the other.

Marple
Greater Manchester

Now that horse-drawn boats are a rarity, grass invades the pavings of a turnover bridge on the Macclesfield canal. Although an entirely practical design, the bridges have a sculptural quality that is artistically satisfying.

THE GRAND CROSS

**Market Drayton
Shropshire**

The end of a perfect day. In the evening sun touring boats lie at their moorings near Tyrley Locks on the Shropshire Union canal. The vigour of Telford's direct, aggressive approach, carving straight routes through the landscape, has been softened by the resurgence of woodland and meadow. The construction of canals caused as much disturbance and provoked as much resistance as the modern motorways, but time has healed the scars.

Running diagonally across the heart of England is a broad, discontinuous valley leading from the Bristol Channel in the south-west to the Humber in the north-east. Birmingham and the surrounding towns sit on a plateau to the north of this valley, with the river Avon below and the valley of the Severn to the west. The valley moves north towards the Mersey and the Cheshire plain, separating the coal-bearing hills to the west from those of the plateau. The Trent, rising in the foothills of the Pennines, runs south towards the plateau before turning north to be joined by the Derwent on its way to the Humber. The south-eastern flank of this valley is formed by the long run of limestone that appears most beautifully in the Cotswolds and continues on and off through the north Oxfordshire wolds towards the Humber and has its final flourish in the North Yorkshire Moors. Draining to the east and to the south of this line are the Nene and the Great Ouse towards the Wash and, cutting through the final barrier to the Thames Valley, the chalk hills of the Chilterns, the Cherwell, which joins the Thames at Oxford. While in the north of England the splendour of the hill country was besmirched with the smoke and fumes of industry, the pleasant rolling countryside of the Midlands found itself host to that byword of industrialization, the Black Country. In a pollution-conscious age the legacy is clear to see, but the inheritance of the canals gives the towns a focus for recovery and leads visitors to unexpected pleasures in the country.

To the south of the Mersey, plans were made as early as 1767 for a canal to run from the Dee at Chester to join the Trent and Mersey canal, which had been started the year before at Middlewich. This soon became derelict, and in the 1790s there was a more ambitious proposal to construct a canal to Shrewsbury on the Severn and to cut across the Wirral from the Dee to the Mersey. Thomas Telford was the engineer of what became the Shropshire Union, though it departed a good deal from the original plan. Branches to the canal would connect with markets and sources of raw materials in the Welsh borders.

The line across the Wirral was completed in 1795 and was soon earning its keep. Work was also started on the centre of the system, around Chirk and Ellesmere, on today's two north Welsh canals, the Llangollen and the Montgomery, but by 1800 plans were changed yet again to take the canal from the end of the Montgomery to the dead branch of the Chester near Nantwich. This was finished in 1805, and the Llangollen became a branch of the system.

To travel from Birmingham, the new industrial centre of England, by way of the Trent and Mersey was to traverse over 80 miles and negotiate 75 locks. In 1826, therefore, the Birmingham and Liverpool Junction was approved (now part of the Shropshire Union) to allow passage as directly as possible from north to south using the Mersey-Chester-Nantwich section now just ticking over, and then ploughing on an almost straight line to Autherley, close to Wolverhampton, to join the network of canals around Birmingham. The distance was reduced to 66 and a half miles and the locks to 45. At the same time, the Macclesfield canal was proposed, and both bear the hallmarks of Telford's robust approach. Where Brindley strove to follow the contour to minimize lockage, Telford used the 'cut and fill' technique. Where the land rose, he sliced deep into the rock, using the spoil to fill the valley and raise embankments, and where that did not suffice, tunnels and aqueducts of unprecedented construction appeared. This was engineering of what we now call Victorian dimensions, and while it may lack the bucolic charm of earlier work, it has a drama that never fails to impress.

Work that had been started at Ellesmere and Chirk on the Llangollen was continued, and the canal was connected to the rest of the system at Nantwich. Once over the Welsh border near Chirk the engineering works are on a scale that can only be justified when the original scheme for a mighty waterway between the Mersey and the Midlands is kept in mind. The River Ceiriog marks the border, running 70 feet below the level of the canal. A massive aqueduct with ten arches spanning 40 feet each was built in stone to overcome the valley. But close by a yet more formidable challenge was to be encountered: the Vale of Llangollen. The Pontcysyllte aqueduct was to span a line 1000 feet long over a drop of 120 feet. To build in stone alone would have demanded a structure on the lines of the great Roman aqueducts like the Pont du Gard, and time and expense would have been prohibitive. Telford and Jessop, whose contribution has been obscured by the fame of his colleague, based their answer on recent developments in the use of metalwork on canals. The earliest aqueducts, such as Brindley's, had supported 'canals in the air', earthworks on top of massive stone piers. The bed of the canal on the Chirk aqueduct had been made from cast-iron plates, but now the entire body of water was to be contained in a metal trough, prefabricated together with its tow-path in cast iron, and the consequent saving in weight permitted the elegant slender stone pillars that astounded observers then and still amaze today. After ten years of building, it opened in 1805.

When the Trent and Mersey canal was in planning, Brindley encouraged the promoters to call it the Grand Trunk, for he saw it as the key to linking the four major seaports of England by means of a Grand Cross of canals. The Trent and Mersey provided the first two arms of the cross, and the third, the Staffordshire and Worcestershire canal to the south-west, he did complete; it opened the year of his death. Three arms of the cross were thus in place, linking the Mersey, Humber and Severn. Only the connection to the Thames was missing, for although his Oxford canal was in the building, there was no connection yet to the northern waterways.

Severn trows had been carrying goods up from the sea to Gloucester, Tewkesbury and further since the Middle Ages. By an Act of Parliament in 1430 it was declared 'common to all the King's people' and thus free of tolls, which could only apply to the tow-paths. Where practicable, the trows sailed, but haulage was necessary where shallows and shifting sandbanks limited navigation, particularly in the upper reaches. The men of Bewdley, for example, relied on their expert knowledge of the uncertain waters to maintain a monopoly of haulage above the town. It was at Bewdley that Brindley intended the Staffordshire and Worcestershire canal to join the river, but the locals would have none of it, so a line along the valley of the Stour was chosen, and the junction with the Severn created an entirely new town.

Stourport is a fascinating example of Georgian town development. Cottages had to be built for the canal workers, and wharves and warehouses needed to handle the transfer of goods from the narrow boats to the trows. A great hotel was constructed, the Tontine, which opened in 1773, a year after the canal itself. By 1820 the town had become 'full of shops and thronged with people' only to face a swift decline, as the Birmingham to Gloucester railway took business from the waterway. As a result the original town survives with far less alteration than more successful locations.

From the northern end, the canal climbs away from the Trent and Mersey to a ten mile level near Wolverhampton and winds down to the Severn without major engineering works being needed. To modern eyes Brindley's work has a particular charm. Even today the engineering achievements are striking, displaying the sympathetic approach to the landscape that makes his canals so attractive. His adherence to the natural contour of the land made for long winding routes, but time was not of the essence in his day, and he held that more people benefited from the waterway as a result. Matured by time, these canals have an ease and peace hard to resist.

The grain of the country could not be less conveniently arranged for the commercial activity of which London is a centre and continental Europe a target. To realize his Grand Cross, James Brindley could contemplate only one route for the arm to London: by the Cherwell valley and the Thames to the south and running east of the Midland plateau to the Trent and Mersey. The Thames itself left a good deal to be desired as a navigation. Water control was in early days by flash locks, single barriers across the river equipped with sluices, known as paddles, that could be raised and lowered to check the flow, and through the gates of which boats either descended like an explorer shooting the rapids or were hauled up by brute force. Pound locks, the two-gated locks with which we are familiar, were introduced between Iffley and Abingdon, near Oxford, in the seventeenth century, but improvements elsewhere were slow to come.

The Bills for the Coventry and Oxford canals were passed in 1768 and 1769. The former joined the Trent and Mersey at its southernmost point, Fradley, and wound away south-east to climb the first step of the limestone ridge north of Nuneaton and then on a level to Coventry. The junction with the Oxford was some five miles before that. The Oxford canal runs south-east from the Hawkesbury-Coventry junction almost on a level until past Rugby it starts a winding southwards climb to the summit of the Oxfordshire Wolds at Fenny Compton. Brindley's contorted route was to be much modified by Vignoles and Cubitt in the 1830s, taking more than 13 miles off the journey from Hawkesbury to Napton with cuttings and embankments. Progress was halted entirely in 1778, when the canal had reached Banbury, a third of the way down the Cherwell valley towards Oxford. Another eight years passed before the work started again, and finally in January 1790 the Grand Cross became a reality.

In the meantime, the development of what was to become a system of over 500 miles of inland waterway around Birmingham had started. The presence of coal and limestone, as well as access to iron ore to the east, spurred the growth of a foul mass of mines, factories and slum dwellings, obscured by a semi-permanent haze of smoke and soot. The perils of pollution, if understood at all, were overlooked in the race for wealth, but it was this wealth that supported the creation not only of the urban canals but of the vital and beautiful ribbons of water that crept across the country to carry raw materials and food-stuffs to the centre of industry and finished goods to the world. The Birmingham canal, running from the Staffordshire and Worcestershire at Autherley, near Wolverhampton, to the town was authorized the same year as the Coventry canal and finished in 1772. This was fine for travel to the north-west, but a roundabout route if the Bristol Channel was the aim. The competition to command trade to the south-west and the west-east movement of goods across the Black Country occupied a great deal of parliamentary time and absorbed a great deal of money in the years to follow. Within the territory grew a mass of waterways, wharves and warehouses. Given that the plateau is actually a series of mounds and dips, canals wove about and flights of locks climbed up and down in a fine confusion that defies concise description.

The Birmingham canal was the first completed adjunct of an existing canal; it connected not to a river, but to the Staffordshire and Worcestershire. Joining one canal with another and building branches to canals to extend their grasp on local trade was the next logical step of development and little of it to the taste of the company first in the field. The challenges of the Stourbridge and the Dudley canals to the Birmingham's grip on the south-west route were eclipsed by an even greater threat in a proposal for a canal from Worcester to Birmingham that would join the Severn twelve miles south of Stourport. This was serious competition for the Birmingham canal's traffic to the Bristol Channel, and the scheme was vigorously resisted. The result was the Worcester Bar; the prohibition of a junction with the older canal at the Birmingham end that was to endure until 1815, subject to which the new project could proceed.

The Worcester and Birmingham route climbs steeply away from the Severn to gain a level for a few miles before meeting a group of locks at Astwood, a mild prelude to the mighty flight of 36 locks at Tardebigge. This brings the waterway to the altitude of 453 feet above sea level, the Birmingham Level at which most of the city's canals are built, and provides a run unencumbered by further locks, passing through the long tunnel at King's Norton on the way. In his autobiography, *Landscape with Canals*, L. T. C. Rolt describes the impact of his first visit:

> The southbound traveller gets no impression of the height of the Birmingham Level until he emerges dramatically from the darkness of the Tardebigge tunnel to find himself floating

along the flank of a hill, a green promontory that juts southward into the blue sea of the vale.

Still another threat to the power of the Birmingham canal appeared in 1793, with the act for the Stratford-upon-Avon canal. The river Avon was already a navigation providing access to the Severn even nearer to its mouth than Worcester, fourteen miles south at Tewkesbury, and the canal would scale the side of the Avon valley to the west, turn north, and climb again to reach the Birmingham Level, some eleven miles from the city by way of a junction with the Worcester and Birmingham at King's Norton. The Warwick and Birmingham, and Warwick and Napton canals (now part of the Grand Union), which gave direct access to the Oxford canal, opened in 1800. The struggling Stratford completed its northern section to join them at Kingswood, where there is physical evidence of the penalties exacted by the established canal on the newcomer. It would have been perfectly practical to join the two canals on the level, for they run side by side. But the connecting arm has been built where the Stratford, the new canal, is at a higher level, so that for every boat that passes between the two, the Warwick and Birmingham gains a lock of water. While business was never up to expectations, the Stratford is a delightful waterway, with curious domed roofs to the lock-keepers' houses, the result of prudent re-use of the formers needed for building the bridges.

To the north and east of Birmingham the broad valley of the Trent leads away to the Humber, and the junction of the river and the Trent and Mersey canal gave birth to another inland port, Shardlow. Ten miles further on, Nottingham marks the southernmost point of the vast coalfields flanking the Pennines and reaching as far as Leeds, while at the same level, enfolded in the end of the dividing range of hills separating east and west, is Derby. To carry manufactures from the towns, and materials to the factories, canals such as the Derby canal and the Erewash down to Nottingham joined the main artery. To the modern eye the purpose of some of these canals is obscure; they appear to run from nowhere in particular to a major thoroughfare. Much has changed since they were busy with laden boats: the mines have been worked out, or their produce is no longer of commercial interest, the quarries fell silent as new materials replaced stone and slate, and once thriving industries have ceased entirely. But the legacy of the waterway remains, here surviving on pleasure traffic, there restored after years of neglect. Often it remains only as an empty channel straddled with redundant bridges overgrown with wildflowers.

At the height of the canal's existence in about 1793, no fewer than 24 Acts of Parliament were passed, and none was more significant for the waterway system than that for the Grand Junction. From the industrial centres of the North and the Midlands, only the Oxford provided access to London, and that by way of a narrow canal and uncertain river navigation. The route to be followed was an ancient one, largely along the Roman road of Watling Street, and is followed today by railway and motorway. From the elbow of the Coventry-Oxford-Birmingham and Warwick complex at Braunston, it runs across the ridges of Northamptonshire to the chalk hills of the Chilterns at Tring, and thence by Rickmansworth and Denham before turning east to the Thames at Brentford. Short canals twigged out along its length to connect such towns as Buckingham, Newport Pagnell, Aylesbury and Wendover, and the Northampton branch gave access to the Nene navigation and thus to the fenlands and the Wash. In the London area another branch ran to Paddington.

Braunston became, and remains, an important centre for boat people. Boat yards and chandlers, a toll-house – now a general store – and the Admiral Nelson, a pub, mark the space between the locks that punctuate the curve of the canal around the village. Standing above it all on a little hill is a church spire and windmill tower. It would seem that this place has long been a crossroads. In the fields to the south-west the ancient ridge and furrow of the deserted village fields of Braunstonbury and Wolfhamcote can be seen, and the latter's church stands alone close to the embankment of the abandoned Daventry-to-Leamington railway and the wandering line of the Oxford canal's former route.

The canal runs to the west to pass through the Braunston tunnel, over a mile long and with a kink in the line to compensate for the error made in the original alignment, before turning south. From this junction a narrow gauge extension, the original Grand Union, heads north, climbing through the Watford Gap, along with the railway and the M1 motorway, towards the Leicestershire and Northamptonshire canal near Market Harborough. The broad canal heads south, where at Gayton an arm leads to the east, eventually to join the Nene near Northampton, and thence to Wellingborough, Peterborough and the sea.

The greatest challenge facing the builders lay between Blisworth and Stoke Bruerne, an ironstone ridge that demanded a great tunnel a mile and three-quarters long. The rest of the canal was completed in 1800, but the first attempt to build Blisworth tunnel failed, and Outram built a horse tramway over the hill. A second attempt at the tunnel was made by Jessop and Barnes, who drove shafts down from above at intervals across the hilltop and hauled the spoil out to be dumped nearby. Going south from Blisworth today, one sees the shafts preserved for ventilation and marked by brick chimneys marching in file across the fields, and low mounds covered with trees are what remain of the spoil heaps. The line of the tramway is also evident. When the task was finally finished in 1805, the tramway was ripped up and rebuilt from Gayton to the Nene to provide a nexus until the Northampton Arm was complete.

As is usual, there is no tow-path through Blisworth tunnel, and in the days of horse-drawn boats the horse was led over the top of the hill while leggers propelled the boat through. On these broad canals they lay on boards projecting over the side of the boat to walk it through the tunnel. In narrow tunnels, which were also lower, they needed no such aids and might even lie on the cargo and push against the roof. The tunnel was dark and wet and very long, but legging provided employment for local men; indeed, it was necessary to have a licence to perform the task. Blisworth men brought boats south, and Stoke Bruerne men waited in The Boat Inn by Stoke top lock to take the northward journey. Then the leggers walked back over the hill to await a new client. With the advent of steam-powered boats and tugs – 'steamers' – leggers became redundant, but the new technology was not without its problems. No one realized what would happen when a steamer attempted the transit. With poor ventilation the available oxygen was in danger of being consumed by the furnace. In the early days at Blisworth a steamer entered the tunnel travelling briskly only to emerge after an unconscionable time, scarcely moving, with the crew of two dead. Additional ventilation shafts were added but too late for those pioneers.

Stoke Bruerne enfolds the canal. Where so many other villages turn their backs on the waterway, here it is a hub of activity. The stone walls of the houses were once overhung with thatch, but today, thanks to economical water transport, Welsh slate provides robust roofing free of fire risks. An old mill, later a warehouse, has been transformed into a museum, and restored boats display their traditional decoration and offer the opportunity to experience the canal from the water.

Below the flight of locks, the Grand Junction traverses the valley of the Great Ouse, thrusting on from Cosgrove over a long embankment and an iron aqueduct above the river itself, and on towards Wolverton. When the canal was first opened, locks lowered the level to that of the river in a temporary arrangement until the time-saving link on one level could be built. The work was given to 'some persons at Stoney Stratford', but only six months after completion the embankment went, and the waters flooded the valley, putting even the citizens of Stony Stratford in fear of their lives. Fortunately, no one was injured, and a local carpenter fashioned a wooden trough to act as a temporary aqueduct until the Ketley Bank Ironworks in Shropshire could deliver the cast-iron structure that remains there to this day.

After winding round the outside of modern Milton Keynes, the long ascent to the top of the Chilterns begins, culminating at Tring. On these chalk hills the provision of sufficient water was a problem met by the construction of large reservoirs, destined to become the delight of thousands of birds and the enthusiasts who take pleasure in watching them. The canal then follows the descent into the Thames valley through Berkhamstead, where the water winds around the old castle mound, Hemel Hempstead, providing a brief distraction for railway passengers. It traverses a pleasant green, past the great paper mills and printing works and through the contrived landscape of Cassiobury Park, where the waterway's design had to please the landowner to gain right of passage. It moves on to Rickmansworth, where so many fine boats were built, and Denham before turning easterly to descend the last twelve locks to the Thames. The former route to Birmingham was over 225 miles: this a mere 138 and a half miles. It was to remain a significant transportation route for over 150 years.

**Chester
Cheshire**

The owner's dog oversees the repainting of a hull in dry dock. This boat is also a home and is an example of the straightforward use of a canal boat as accommodation. A television aerial has been fitted, the dustbin secured against passing jokers, and the cooking arrangements are practical rather than traditional. The paintwork is simply serviceable. The conventional tiller of a powered boat is entirely without the 'twisting', the barber's pole helical stripes that grace crafts of classic style.

**Chester
Cheshire**

Chester is an important port in the canal system with maintenance facilities that are still in use today. Most modern boats are steel-hulled, and rust is kept at bay by welding a sacrificial zinc anode to the hull.

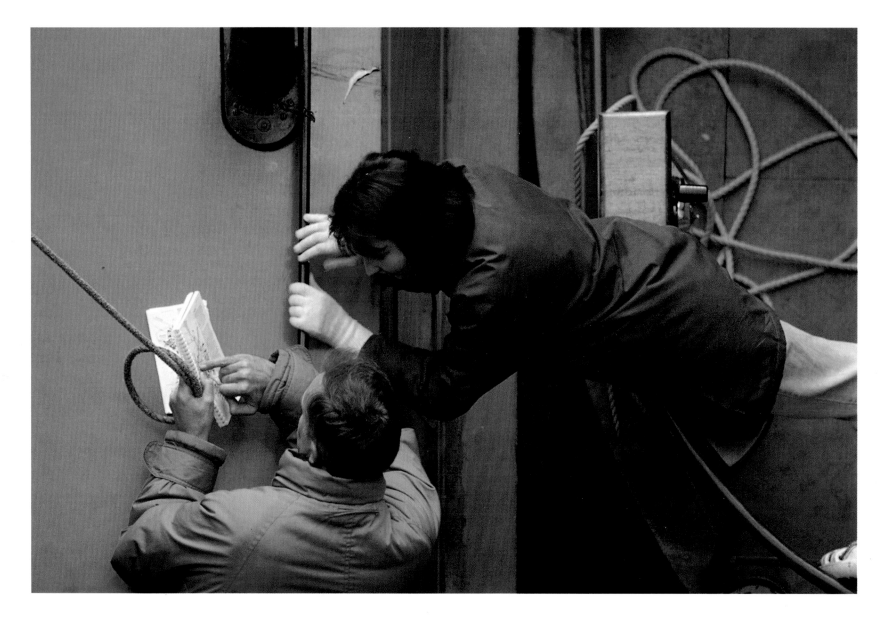

Chester
Cheshire

A chance meeting at a lock permits an exchange of information
on the route ahead. The navigable waterways are well covered
by guides and maps for travellers
by boat or on foot.

Chester
Cheshire

Northgate Locks, Nos. 41, 42
and 43 on the Shropshire Union
Canal. These locks form a staircase; the lower gates of one
chamber are the upper gates of
the next. This structure allows
the canal to lift sharply in a short
distance, but it has the disadvantage of using a lot of water and
making it impossible for boats to
pass each other.

Whitchurch
Shropshire

On its long journey from Nantwich to the Welsh mountains, the Llangollen canal passes from the gentle hills of Cheshire to the boggy country of Whixall Moss. This canal was originally conceived as part of the ambitious plan to create a major waterway from Ellesmere Port on the Mersey, via Chester, to the Severn at Shrewsbury, but instead of driving on south from Frankton, it was built north-east to Nantwich to become, with the Montgomery, part of a two-canal offshoot of the Shropshire Union. In these peaceful lowlands a boat lies comfortably at her mooring.

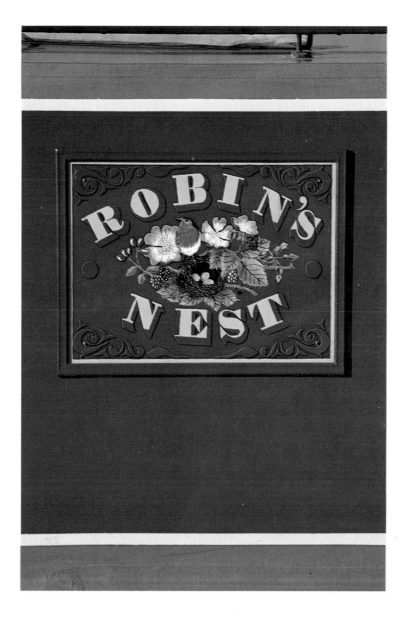

**Ellesmere
Shropshire**

A modern name plate preserves the traditional spirit of decoration on the canal boat, although the style is original. Dog roses, fruit and a Robin with its nest are all unusual motifs but neatly pun the name of the boat.

Whitchurch
Shropshire

The Low Country character of the Llangollen Canal as it crosses Whixall Moss is emphasized by a modern lift bridge that recalls a Van Gogh painting. Canals cut farms in two, and the provision of accommodation bridges was an expense the builders could not avoid. They used local materials – stone, brick or wood – as the case might be. With changes of ownership of the land and the introduction of massive machinery, many accommodation bridges have become redundant but may still be seen going from nowhere to nowhere.

**Ellesmere
Shropshire**

In the heart of the Shropshire
Lake District lies Ellesmere,
close to the junction of the
Llangollen and Montgomery
canals. The warehouse suitable
to a prosperous commercial centre dominates the waterfront.
The building of the canal
between here and Chirk was
undertaken at a time when this
was to be a stage on the route to
Shrewsbury, a scheme that was
not fulfilled. Nonetheless, there
was enough business in agricultural products and materials for
the modified plan to be economic, if not quite profitable.

**Ellesmere
Shropshire**

Modern holiday boats are
moored snugly in the basin. The
Montgomery canal towards
Welshpool and Newtown is
being made navigable once
more, but the main attraction
of the area is the route towards
Llangollen, where some of the
most striking engineering
achievements, not merely of the
canal age but in all of Britain,
are to be seen.

**Ellesmere
Shropshire**

A secure mooring in early spring
near the town. The cabin stove
is going well, and there is plenty
of fuel to hand; logs for the stove
lie conveniently on the cabin
top. Roof-leeks flourish in a
selection of containers, including modern flower-pots decorat-
ed with traditional narrow-boat
rose motifs.

Chirk
Clwyd, Wales

A boat from Wales glides through the cutting on the approach to the Chirk Tunnel as evening approaches, its headlight ready for the underground voyage. Other boats have already decided to call it a day, and drifting smoke suggests warm cabins in the cool of early spring. Chirk Tunnel, some 450 yards long, was built complete with a towpath, now protected by an iron rail. Tow-paths were not provided in earlier tunnels; building them was sufficient challenge without adding to their size. Boats were propelled through by 'legging', men on the boat walking along the walls or roof. On broad canals, boards were fixed overhanging the side of the boat on which the men lay, while on narrow canals they lay on the cargo or the deck. Walkers at Chirk should take care, as the path is uneven and the rail of uncertain strength.

Froncysyllte
Clwyd, Wales

The innovative solution to spanning the Dee valley was the prefabrication of the entire upper part of the Pontcysyllte aqueduct. Designed by Telford and Jessop, it had iron sections that create a light, delicate form, in contrast to the previous massive structures at Chirk. The stone pillars are hollow towards the top to make a further saving in weight. The tow-path is part of the alternate route of the Offa's Dyke long-distance path which turns north at the far end by Trevor Wharf, from which the never built continuation of the waterway was intended to make its way to Wrexham, Chester and the Mersey.

**Fronsycyllte
Clwyd, Wales**

Floating 120 feet above the
River Dee, the Pontcysyllte
aqueduct has a tow-path and
railing to one side, and just the
narrow edge of the channel on
the other side. L. T. C. Rolt
observed in *Landscape with
Canals*: 'from my position at the
tiller I had an uninterrupted
view up the Vale of Llangollen
towards the ancient Welsh
fortress of Castell Dynas Bran
that guards the little town. On
this brilliant, cloudless June day,
the valley floor was most richly
green while the more distant
hills basked in a shimmering
haze of heat.'

**Froncysyllte
Clwyd, Wales**

A century and a half ago artists
were swift to praise great works
of engineering. Robert Southey
wrote of the builder:

TELFORD who o'er the vale of
  Cambrian Dee
Aloft in air at giddy height
  upborne
Carried his Navigable road. . .

Llangollen
Clwyd, Wales

Today horse-drawn boats carry visitors to the Llangollen canal, but barges on the river navigations were often drawn by men. On the Severn, for example, the men of Bewdley specialized in hauling traffic up the river's shoaling and changeable waters and refused to cooperate with the new canals for fear of losing their monopoly. Canals were built with tow-paths specifically to overcome right-of-way problems experienced on the river-banks, and horse power endured until steam and later the internal combustion engine took over.

**Ellesmere
Shropshire**

A sign bears witness to the changes of canal ownership. Railway companies acquired them not only for the use of the routes they had pioneered, but also to divert their traffic to the benefit of the trains. The railway companies themselves were not immune to takeover. The London, Midland and Scottish Railway – the LMS – has swallowed the Shropshire in order to establish a hold in a competitor's territory. Nowadays a licence to cycle the tow-path can be obtained from British Waterways.

Chirk
Clwyd, Wales

The decoration typical of the narrow boat is often likened to that of the gypsy caravan, but no connection has ever been demonstrated. Castles, roses and energetic flourishes are traditional motifs for canal boats and appear where the steerer of the boat could enjoy them. This 'pigeon box', an engine room ventilator, is embellished with coloured triangles and a romantic waterside castle.

Pipe-clayed rope-work, only some of it functional, is a typical form of decoration found on canal boats. This particular design is called a 'Turk's Head'.

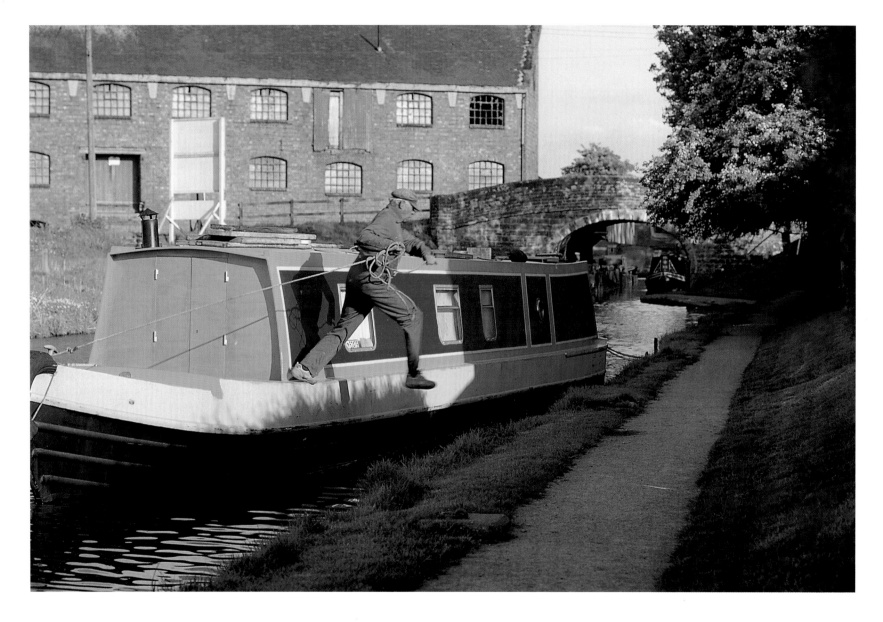

**Market Drayton
Shropshire.**

Under the gaze of an old warehouse, a nimble boatman moors.
The bow 'strap', or mooring line,
looks ready to give problems.

**Market Drayton
Shropshire**

The unmistakable autograph of
Telford in the Shropshire Union
Canal. Straight as an arrow, the
canal speeds vessels across the
landscape. Unlike Brindley, who
avoided locks and earthworks as
much as possible, Telford was
heir to the traditions of John
Smeaton and William Jessop,
builders of river navigations and
broad canals. For them, the lay
of the land was something to
be overcome.

**Market Drayton
Shropshire**

The canals brought coal to the
open farmlands of Shropshire.
Although the fuel yard is now
separated from the canal by
rough wooden fencing, the business founded on water transport
survives, supplied by roads.
Farming was evolving as swiftly
as industry at the time the canals
were built. Lime and sand for
soil improvement were carried
by water, as was manure, which
threatened to overwhelm the
towns served by horse-drawn
carriages.

**Market Drayton
Shropshire**

Though often neglected, the
canal-side buildings of the late
eighteenth and early nineteenth
centuries are another pleasure
along the waterways, both in
their overall aspect and in their
details. As utilitarian a feature as
an air vent on a warehouse is
worthy of fine design.

**Market Drayton
Shropshire**

Approaching Tyrley Locks on
the Shropshire Union. The pale
stone archway set into the brick
bridge aids twilight navigation.
Beneath the bridge, steps offer
the boatman access to the lock-
side, and next to the tow-path
an iron guard-plate protects the
brickwork from damage by grit-
encrusted tow-ropes.

**Market Drayton
Shropshire**

In the evening light workboats lie quietly on the Shropshire Union. The canal strides across the fields on an embankment, while a weir regulates the water level.

**Market Drayton
Shropshire**

Tyrley Locks on the Shropshire Union. To the left of the gates is the by-wash, which allows excess water to drain past the lock. The flow of water in a canal can make for difficulty, as the length of a narrow boat is as hard to handle in a cross-current as it is in a cross-wind. The boat can be turned across the waterway and can get jammed. The Tyrley flight is approached through a typical Telford cutting, straight as a die through the rock. 'Cut and fill' were the watchwords. The direct line was preserved as far as possible, tunnelling or cutting through rising land and filling in the declivities with embankments or aqueducts. Locks were grouped in flights to permit continuous running on the long pounds in between. The construction work was done by hundreds of 'navigators' or 'navvies' wielding picks and shovels and carting the spoil off by wheelbarrow. Cheap and plentiful labour was a prerequisite of canal building.

Stoke-on-Trent
Staffordshire

The Trent and Mersey canal was promoted by Josiah Wedgwood to provide transportation for raw materials to, and finished goods from, his pottery plant. The bottle kilns used to fire the product survive along the canal at Stoke amongst the clutter of more recent industry.

Cheddleton
Staffordshire

The cabin and rudder of *Vienna*. The shapes of the rudder and tiller reveal that it is a butty boat – an unpowered boat towed by horse or another boat. Pipe-clayed rope-work adorns the rudder, castles and roses the doors, and the Fellows, Morton & Clayton livery the cabin.

**Cheddleton
Staffordshire**

Vienna has a castle motif on the cabin block directly in the steerer's line of sight. The cargo space of the boat is covered with a tarpaulin stretched over top planks, which are in turn supported by vertical timbers or stands and rest astern on the cabin block.

**Cheddleton
Staffordshire**

In a cabin like the *Vienna*'s, measuring about 7 by 10 feet, a whole family would eat, sleep and raise their children. The cupboard, painted with traditional motifs, conceals a fold-down double-bed for the parents. Children's bunks serve as daytime seating. Lighting is by oil lamp, and memories of earlier years are recalled in a framed photograph.

**Cheddleton
Staffordshire**

An old hoist stands on the wharf beside the Caldon, with the authentic butty boat *Vienna* moored beyond.

**Cheddleton
Staffordshire**

The remains of a plate tramway. Tramways were used to move materials to the canals or to fill the gaps in waterway systems during their construction. The plates (rails) are flanged, but the wheels of the wagon are not, a configuration that was reversed in the development of railways. Here, the plates are mounted on wooden sleepers. It was more usual to fasten them to stone blocks, and where the plates are no longer in place the fastening holes can still be found.

**Cheddleton
Staffordshire**

The Caldon branch of the Trent and Mersey climbs away from Stoke into the countryside, with the southern arm leading to Froghall. The flint mill at Cheddleton was built by the versatile Brindley to grind flint to powder, raw material for shipment to the potteries of Stoke.

**Cheddleton
Staffordshire**

Structural efficiency leads to the elegant simplicity of a stone bridge over the Caldon canal.

Horse Bridge
Staffordshire

The Caldon arm of the Trent and Mersey forks at Hazelhurst, and the Froghall route drops to the valley. The Leek branch clings to the hillside to pass over its companion by way of a fine aqueduct. This early Victorian structure features white-painted brick where smaller bridges use local stone.

Horse Bridge
Staffordshire

A fine wide causeway on the top of the Hazelhurst aqueduct. From this vantage point the visitor has a wonderful view of the Froghall branch making its way along the tight little valley past a pub and under steep little bridges.

**Stourport-on-Severn
Hereford and Worcester**

Before the coming of the
Staffordshire and Worcestershire
canal – the south-western arm
of Brindley's Grand Cross –
there was no town here at all;
Stourport is a creation of the
new transport network. The
canal company undertook a
complete town-building pro-
gramme, from workers' cottages,
warehouses and boat-repair facilities to luxury accommodation
for travellers and officials. Goods
brought down from Birmingham
and the North were traded and
shipped for the Bristol Channel
and the markets of the world.
An equally lively trade in the
opposite direction supplied the
factories of the Black Country
with raw materials.

Stourport-on-Severn
Hereford and Worcester

The elegant warehouse beside the basin at Stourport is crowned by a delicate clock tower. When the canal trade declined in the mid-nineteenth century, the town came to depend on tourism for survival. Families would escape the smoke and fumes of the Black Country to enjoy the style and freshness of this Severnside resort.

**Stourport-on-Severn
Hereford and Worcester**

Within a half-century of its foundation during the flowering Georgian period, railways were diverting business from Stourport, and the town ceased to be of importance as a commercial entrepôt. The result is an unspoilt Georgian town preserved largely as it stood in the early nineteenth century.

**Stourport-on-Severn
Hereford and Worcester**

The Tontine, the great hotel constructed in Stourport, was opened in 1773. Built as a hotel rather than an inn, it stood amongst smooth lawns to suggest a certain standing. It provided rooms for extended occupancy, as well as for a simple overnight stop. With the decline of the canal, it had been divided into twenty separate residences by 1842. Named after its inventor, the Italian banker Lorenzo Tonti, a 'tontine' is a financial system in which the share of a holder who dies is divided amongst the survivors, and continues thus until the whole annuity goes to the last one remaining. .

Stourport-on-Severn
Hereford and Worcester

It was planned to join the Staffordshire and Worcestershire canal to the Severn at Bewdley, but locals rejected any association with Brindley's 'stinking ditch', and the junction was made four miles south. This broad lock allowed the river boats, Severn trows, to enter the basin to transfer loads to narrow boats. The narrow locks for the canal boats are nearby. During the easy years of prosperity locks were worked only in daylight hours, but as rival transport increased they came to be open 24 hours a day. The locks were also the places at which tolls were collected, and the function of the lock-keeper was not to fill or empty the chamber – the boatmen did that – but to gather fees. In February 1832 the Stourport keeper was paid 14/- (£0.70) a week plus 4/- (£0.20) for night duty.

Wooten Wawen
Warwickshire

Above the road to Henley-in-
Arden at Wooten Wawen an
iron-channelled aqueduct carrying the Stratford canal is supported on piers of brick, the local
building material. A visiting boat
from the Nene navigation slides
past the pub at roof level.

Wooten Wawen
Warwickshire

Next to the Wooten Wawen
aqueduct stands the Navigation
Inn. Boatmen's pubs were not
always named so aptly, but all
provided vital services to those
who worked on the canals. Just
like the coaching inns of former
times, there was stabling for
horses, refreshment and a meeting place for the peripatetic com-
munity of canal-goers. The sign-
painter has invented a hybrid
boat – a butty, from the tiller and
rudder, but powered by steam.

**Wilmcote
Warwickshire**

One of the Stratford's characteristic split bridges. Supported by
stout brickwork piers, the bridge
is divided into two halves, allowing the tow-rope to be passed
through the centre split without
casting it off from the boat.

Wilmcote
Warwickshire

The Stratford-upon-Avon canal was planned to take a share of the busy trade away from the centre of heavy industry, Birmingham, with its export markets reached by way of the River Severn and the Bristol Channel. By the time it was built, however, the canal to Worcester had seized the bulk of the business. Still, the Stratford remains one of England's prettiest canals.

Lapworth
Warwickshire

The lock-keeper's cottages on the Stratford are unique in their curious curved roofs. An economy measure, the rafters are the recycled formers that were used for building bridge arches over the waterway.

Stratford-upon-Avon
Warwickshire

At Stratford-upon-Avon canal boats followed the navigation down to Tewkesbury on the River Severn and thence to the seaport of Bristol. Today commercial boating is predominantly of the hired-by-the-hour variety for the enjoyment of the old town's beauty, with its stone bridges and the elegant swans of the Avon.

Stratford-upon-Avon
Warwickshire

A skiff evokes an age of gentle recreations, though not free from regulation. The licence plate is fixed to the transom of this boat, limiting the number of passengers it may carry.

Stratford-upon-Avon Warwickshire

Moored rowing skiffs invite visitors to a sunny afternoon just messing about on the river. Of the many thousands of visitors who make the pilgrimage to Shakespeare's birthplace, only a few explore further than the obvious sites, and still fewer discover the canal that joins the Avon here.

Birmingham

The old brick factories and warehouses that line the banks of the Birmingham canals fell into dereliction in the twentieth century, but an increasing appreciation of their beauty is leading to their restoration rather than their demolition, as well as to their use for business and pleasure.

Birmingham

The canal's reinstatement is evident at Farmer's Bridge Locks (the 'Old 13') and here at Gas Street Basin, the site of one of the waterway's great curiosities – Worcester Bar. When the Worcester and Birmingham Act was passed in 1791, it contained a clause forbidding any connection by water with the Birmingham canal, the owners of which feared a loss of business from their line to the newcomer. Thus, although the new canal was built to terminate at Gas Street Basin, it was separated from the city's waterways by a bank of land, a physical bar, onto which cargo had to be unloaded and loaded afresh for onward carriage. The situation persisted until 1815. Use of the canals for carriage of cargo has not entirely ceased. A powerful little boat pushes a coal boat on the Birmingham canal.

**Grafton Regis
Northamptonshire**

The village where Henry VIII
courted Anne Boleyn overlooks
the Northamptonshire countryside. Today, canal boats make
their way towards Stoke Bruerne
on the Grand Union canal.

**Grafton Regis
Northamptonshire**

On her annual run up the Grand
Union is the last of the steamers,
President, with the butty boat
Kildare close astern. The angled
tiller distinguishes the powered
boat. On this special occasion
the boatman is dressed according
to the old custom in corduroy
trousers, waistcoat and cap, with
a bright scarf at his neck.

**Marsworth
Hertfordshire**

From the central canal of the
Grand Union, branches reach
out to such destinations as
Buckingham, Newport Pagnell,
Wendover and Aylesbury. The
single top gate on the Aylesbury
arm shows that the branch was
built narrow, while the main
line was broad. The branch
joins the main canal near Tring,
approaching the top of the climb
over the Chilterns, where reservoirs made to ensure the water
supply now support an enthusi-
ast's paradise of wild birds.
Even the timbers of the gates
and sluices offer footholds
for wildlife.

THE SOUTHERN ROUTES TO LONDON

Bath
Avon

Robert Adam's Pulteney Bridge
was completed in 1774. The
pavilions at either end were originally toll-houses. The weir
marks the transition of the Avon
from river to navigation, part of
the works necessary to the control of the water level for commercial traffic.

London, the political and commercial capital of England, is surrounded on three sides by hills and open to the sea in the east. For centuries London's river, the Thames, was the sole substantial route for commerce, both domestic and foreign. The great wedge of clay upon which London stands is squeezed from the north by the chalk hills of the Chilterns, which are interrupted by the Goring Gap – through which the Thames passes south from Oxford – and continue in the Berkshire and Malborough Downs, merging with the open heathlands of Salisbury Plain. The southern side runs from there through the Hampshire Downs, is cut by the river Wey, and swings around in the form of the barrier of the North Downs to end abruptly in the dramatic white cliffs of Dover; the South Downs move from Hampshire closer to the sea, terminating at Beachy Head. To the west of this chalk bastion a clay valley separates it from the long diagonal of limestone that forms the Cotswolds and gives way to the basin of the Severn and the Bristol Channel.

The hills around London presented travellers on land with problems. The chalk provided good routes; indeed, in prehistoric times the Ridgeway was a highroad from Norfolk to the Dorset coast. But once off the chalk, going north or west, there was trouble. Quite apart from the struggle to climb the hills, the descent brought the traveller to poor roads on clay, which were swiftly mired up in wet weather. Although the turnpike roads eased the difficulties, bulk goods were expensive and troublesome to convey.

Sea transport did not provide a complete solution either. The routes were long and hazardous; in times of peace they involved the dangerous rounding of Cornwall's rocky coasts and the shoaling waters off Kent, and in war they were additionally threatened by enemy action. With Bristol a major trading port and London of supreme importance, an inland east-west link had obvious attractions.

For traders in the Thames valley, the river gave access to the markets of the capital, an opportunity envied by residents near the tributaries. Sir Richard Weston, who lived at Sutton Place near Guildford, was troubled by the regular flooding of the Wey, and sought to solve the problem and create good business by making the river navigable down to the Thames. A scheme he proposed was approved by Charles I but delayed by the Civil War. The benefits for Guildford after its completion were reported by Daniel Defoe in the 1720s:

> The river which . . . is call'd the Wey, and which falls into the Thames at Oatlands, is made navigable to this town, which adds greatly to its trade; and by this navigation a very great quantity of timber is brought down to London . . . This navigation is also a mighty support to the great corn-market at Farnham.

Defoe was a strong advocate of road improvement and argued for the establishment of turnpikes throughout the country. Others compared the ease with which bulk cargoes were handled on the river navigations with the misery on the highways, and could see the advantages of extending canals from the navigations. By branching off from the Wey quite close to the Thames, a canal could be run to Basingstoke, on the edge of the chalk uplands and the better roads of the Hampshire Downs, and thence west towards Bristol. It was an idea unattractive to the citizens of Reading who feared the loss of trade to the west by the Kennet and Newbury. But just as important was the impact expected on agriculture, which was in a state of revolutionary development equal to that of industry. The improvement of the land by using manure, lime and sea sand was newly realized, but transporting these materials was expensive. The canal was expected to cut the cost by more than 90 per cent.

The Basingstoke Canal obtained its act during the War of American Independence, which slowed progress on the ground, but the canal eventually opened in 1794. The effect on farming and the businesses of Basingstoke was precisely as desired. The timing of its opening just as the French Revolutionary Wars started supported the canal for a while, as goods were being sent inland to Southampton and Portsmouth instead of running the risk of enemy action in the Channel. But with peace in 1815 and the burden of servicing the debts with which the canal opened, a long decline set in until the railways finished it off.

The Wey and Arun canal fared even worse. The plan was simply to link the prosperous Wey navigation to the Channel by joining the Arun, south of the Weald, and thereby taking boats past the ancient castle at Arundel down to the sea. An old idea, it gained impetus from the French wars but obtained its act only two years before the end of hostilities and opened three years after. It suffered from a problem common to all southern canals – lack of water. Because the waterway passed over porous chalk hills, leakage constantly had to be fought, and what rainfall there was, about half of that of the Pennines, soaked away quickly, necessitating reservoirs and pumping stations. And again came the railway. The power of steam, which had earlier concentrated industry and encouraged the canals, now lent speed to overland travel and reliability to sea shipping.

In the late 1860s J. B. Dashwood made a voyage from the Thames to the Solent in his Una boat *Caprice*. He found the Wey and Arun a challenge.

> On opening the lock we saw to our horror and dismay that there was scarcely a foot of water in the Canal. We pushed and punted along and carried away our towing rope in our efforts, and thus managed to gain about a hundred yards, when we stuck fast. What was to be done? . . . The man now made his appearance, and . . . said he could get us more water, but that it would be a very expensive affair. After a while half-a-crown smoothed matters.

The extension of river navigations to conquer the east-west route could be achieved in two places: from the headwaters of the Thames, west of Oxford, or from the Kennet navigation at Newbury. The former would have to cross the limestone ridge of the Cotswolds, and the latter would have to deal with the chalk downs. Various schemes were mooted from the time of Elizabeth I onwards, but it was not until 1779, when the Stroudwater canal brought regular shipping up from the Severn to Stroud, the centre of the cloth trade, that a practical opportunity arose. The Thames and Severn canal was authorized four years later to join the new navigation by the Frome river valley, which cuts deep into the hills east of Stroud, then through a long tunnel to emerge on the gentle slopes to the south of Cirencester, and on to the Thames near Lechlade.

The Frome valley is one of the Cotswold's most dramatic landscapes. The wide uplands stand some 700 feet above sea level, and from them the valley plunges some 500 feet down steep tree-clad hillsides to a little ribbon of water bordered by mills and houses of mellow stone and fertile meadows. This is the Golden Valley, where the manufacture of cloth made fortunes before the great industrial centres of the north took over the trade. The canal reached Chalford in 1785 and Daneway a year later, hard by the workings of the Sapperton tunnel, which gave real problems to the engineer, Robert Whitworth and his assistant, Josiah Clowes. Over two miles long, it was drilled for much of its length through solid rock that required no lining but an enormous expenditure of energy. The first boat passed through the tunnel in the spring of 1789, and by the winter traffic was making the complete journey to and from the Thames.

The still unsolved problem was leakage, much of it within the tunnel at the top level. In *Landscape with Canals* L. T. C. Rolt recounts the experience of Charles Ballinger, a Gloucester boatman, who as a young man had worked with his father on the canal:

He would shake his head over the chronic shortage of water on the summit of the Thames and Severn. So bad was it that, in the canal's last days, the company provided what he called 'lightening boats' at each end of the great summit tunnel at Sapperton. He and his father used to offload part of their cargo into a lightening boat before setting out laboriously to 'leg' their way through the two-miles-long tunnel, towing the smaller boat behind them which, of course, had to be unloaded again into their own boat at the tunnel's end. But, as he pointed out, anything was better than being stuck on the bottom in those dark depths.

This water shortage, combined with the not uncommon defects in the management of the company's finances and the poor state of the upper waters of the Thames, limited the canal's development and rendered it vulnerable to the competition that came from the other great canal to the south. Today the legacy of the Thames and Severn is to be seen in the appearance of Stroud. There, in a country dominated by stone, are brick dwellings – the result of boatmen finding loads for their return journey to the west after bringing cloth east to the Thames valley's claylands.

The Kennet, which joins the Thames at Reading, was authorized as a navigation in 1715. Until then, Reading had enjoyed the benefit of being a trading outlet for the towns on and beyond the downs to the west and south. Hence, the development of the navigation and the increased importance of Newbury, to which it ran, was resisted, at times with violent riots. Even after it opened in 1723, threats were issued against the men working the new route:

> Redding July 10 [1725]. Mr Darvall wee Bargemen of Redding thought to Aquaint you
> before 'tis too Late, Dam You, if y. work a bote any more to Newbery wee will Kill You if you
> ever come again this way, wee was very near shooting you last time, wee went with pistolls
> and was not too Minnets too Late.

The valley of the Kennet is very beautiful, gentle country, with willows and watermills beside the placid stream. The mill owners were also opposed to the navigation, fearing a lack of water to drive their machinery, and they too took extreme action to combat the boatmen. Water was diverted, crowds gathered, stones were thrown, and conflict threatened until compensation was paid belatedly to those whose trade was harmed.

Pushing on west from Newbury was proposed, and the serious work of surveying carried out in 1789. The results were scrutinized by Robert Whitworth, engineer of the Thames and Severn, who after some bitter experiences questioned the availability of water. Young John Rennie was appointed to re-survey the route and found no such problem. Money was easily raised, and in 1794 the necessary act was passed. It was a massive undertaking. From Reading to Newbury, the Kennet navigation lifted boats some 120 feet, but to attain the long level through the pleasant Vale of Pewsey to Devizes, a summit another 200 feet up had to be overcome. Devizes itself stands on the edge of the Malborough Downs, and the valley of the Avon, the way to Bath, is 300 feet below.

Water supply, in the event, was a problem. Rennie had to construct a reservoir, Wilton Water, near Crofton, just below the summit, to collect water from the natural springs and make it available for pumping up to the top level. A pumping station was constructed at Crofton, and a Boulton and Watt beam engine, built in 1801, installed. It had a 36-inch bore and eight-foot stroke, slightly smaller than the 42-inch bore engine that joined it in 1813 and is there to this day.

While the canal was in construction, the centre section was furnished with the usual temporary tramway to the foot of the largest obstacle, Caen Hill. Today, the approach to Devizes by car from the west involves a relatively trivial climb up the flank of the Malborough Downs to the town. From the valley floor and to the left of the road, there is what appears to be a broad unkempt field with a dirty stripe up one edge. Up close, the stripe resolves itself into a series of deep locks and their 16 side ponds, which form the middle section of the 29-lock Devizes flight rising some 240 feet.

Further west the Avon cuts through the Cotswolds on its way to Bath, forming a steep and winding wooded valley with fresh challenges for Rennie. The canal runs embanked high above the river, lodged against the hillside. The artificial waterway is vulnerable to slippage of the earthworks, at best causing leaks and a total collapse of the bank at worst. These troubles persist today, and concrete lining is being used in an attempt to effect permanent repairs. Below the delightful old town of Bradford-on-Avon, with its stone buildings cascading down the cluttered hillside, the gorge narrows, and the river, canal and railway all vie for space, leaving little room for the road. On reaching Avoncliff the canal is forced to change to the other side of the valley, passing over a handsome aqueduct, aged and a little bent, that looks down on the mills and cottages built here long before the navigators came. The town pub stands prudently clear of river floods, with its back pressed against the tow-path; indeed, its lower windows were closed up when the ballast creating the canal bank was dumped.

A few miles further on what must be one of the finest aqueducts in the land carries the canal back across the river. The Dundas aqueduct is a noble work in the same style as its sister at Avoncliffe but, in the slightly more open valley, much more impressive. From Dundas down water was still insufficient, and another pumping station, water-powered, was built at Claverton.

Bath, that elegant spa, inspires thoughts of Roman remains, Beau Nash and the disapproval of Jane Austen – not at all the natural setting for a great artery of commerce. Visitors to Sydney Gardens stroll in peace beside quiet waters, quite unaware that this is the Kennet and Avon canal, bridged and landscaped to accord with the tastefulness of its surroundings.

London, the target of so much of this effort, was itself to be furnished with its own waterways, in part for the supply of the metropolis and in part to give access to the Port of London and the sea. The Grand Junction reached the Thames at Brentford in 1794, but eastbound traffic was then limited to the Thames itself. In order to obtain more trade, an arm was built and completed seven years later from Bull's Bridge Junction in Southall through the open country to Paddington, then on the edge of the town. The final connection to the Docklands at Limehouse Basin was not made until 1829, when the Regent's Canal was finished. The construction of a new canal so close to the centre of government and commerce excited great interest, and a fine engraving of the mouth of the Islington Tunnel appeared in The Gentleman's Magazine of August 1819 with a comment from a certain 'TB':

> The Tunnel formed for the Regent's Canal, under the hill at Pentonville, in the parish of Islington, having excited a considerable degree of public curiosity, I request you to insert in your useful Miscellany a View of its Mouth, surmounted with a prospect of the celebrated Tea-house called White Conduit House . . .
>
> Some years ago, this house and premises were kept by Mr Christopher Bartholomew, who was reduced from a state of affluence and respectability to wretchedness and want by gambling in the State Lotteries. His melancholy fate is held out as a warning to others . . .

> After passing through the Regent's Park, and there forming supplies for the ornamental lakes of water in the Park, it runs nearly in a straight direction across the Hampstead and Kentish-town roads to the tunnel . . . From the Eastern end of the tunnel the line passes along pasturage-fields to the inn called the Rosemary-branch; a little to the Westward of which, a branch will be taken off, and carried across the City-road (over which will be erected a handsome bridge); and the canal then proceeds . . . to the Mile-end-road, across the Commercial-road; and finally terminates in the North bank of the Thames at Limehouse, being altogether a distance of 8 3/4 miles . . . The whole line is now so nearly complete, that it is expected to be opened in a few months.

The optimism about the speed of construction was unfounded, and what the fate of Mr Bartholomew has to do with the canal is obscure, but the relationship between town and country and pleasure park and commercial waterway described here is timeless.

Having heavy goods transported through a town was then, as now, not without its dangers. In 1874 there was a huge explosion in Regent's Park when a boat 'laden with petroleum and gunpowder for blasting' blew up. It was just going under Macclesfield Bridge, the road bridge to the west of the zoo. The blast destroyed the structure entirely and damaged nearby houses. Windows were broken in houses up to a mile away, and the sound was heard all over London. When the bridge was rebuilt, the iron supporting columns were replaced, and they were turned 180 degrees so that the grooves worn by the grit-covered tow-ropes before the accident appear on the side away from the canal. Boat people call the bridge Blow-up Bridge to this day. Legislation regulating the carriage of dangerous goods was not long in following.

After years of neglect the canals, both in town and country, are appreciated anew. In London, Little Venice is an area of calm and beauty that comes as a surprise so close to the traffic pounding along the raised thoroughfare of Westway. In Birmingham, Gas Street Basin and the Old 13 lie peaceful within yards of the frenzy of modern commerce. In the mellow lowlands of the Midlands, the chalk uplands of the South and the harsh hills of the North, the waterways wind across the country, bringing walkers and holiday boaters closer to the past and to a present more attuned to the natural world.

Sutton Green
Surrey

Before the Civil War, Sir Richard Weston of Sutton Place, near Guildford, obtained the approval of Charles I to turn the troublesome River Wey into a navigation, thus protecting his property from flood and drought and encouraging commerce. Daniel Defoe reported in the 1720s: 'the meal-men and other dealers but the corn at [Farnham], much of it is brought to the mills on this river; which is not above seven miles distant, and being first ground and dress'd, is sent down in the meal by barges to London, the expense of which is very small'.

Sutton Green
Surrey

The character of the Wey navigation contrasts strongly with the robust environment of the northern canals. Rich landowners insisted that navigations and canals be tailored to enhance their property, even at the cost of making a less efficient waterway for commerce.

**Sutton Green
Surrey**

An ordered countryside along the Wey. Artfully planted trees give the impression of natural-ness only achieved by the skill of the landscape architect.

**Sutton Green
Surrey**

Practical considerations, the pro-tection of the brickwork from straying boats, led to the seating of a stout post to guard the pier of the bridge. A poem in colour and texture results.

**Sutton Green
Surrey**

Softly through the Surrey landscape, the Wey now serves recre-
ation rather than commerce.

**Sutton Green
Surrey**

Throughout England the waterways provide habitats for
wildlife. Even common birds,
such as these mallards, are a
delight to see.

**Deepcut
Surrey**

The poor soils of the Surrey-Hampshire border country support beautiful woodlands. It was to improve the soil for farming and to speed delivery of produce that the Basingstoke canal was built. For a period during the Napoleonic Wars, it served as part of an inland route from London to the naval installations at Portsmouth, but peace threw the waterway back on the slender agricultural trade, which was unable to sustain it for long.

**Deepcut
Surrey**

After many years of neglect the route is once more open to boats. Ironically, protests have been made that their passage disturbs the peace and security of the wildlife, in spite of the fact that without the canal this environment would not exist at all.

**Deepcut
Surrey**

Around the lock-keeper's cottage, with its dry dock alongside, is the evidence of the continuous work required to keep the canal in good order. The growth of weeds in the water is controlled by paddle boats, which tear out the plants as they pass.

**Deepcut
Surrey**

A cheerful lengthman on the Basingstoke canal. He is responsible for the maintenance of a given stretch of the waterway, deals with commonplace problems, and alerts higher authority should major works be required. Although it is rare, it is not unknown for embankments on canals to break, exposing local people to the risks of floods. The vigilance of the lengthman is thus crucial.

Bath
Avon

The Kennet and Avon canal wraps around the south of the town, climbing away from the Avon along the hillside and affording fine views of the Georgian buildings.

BATH HUMANE SOCIETY'S STATION.

FOR LIFEBUOYS & DRAG-POLES

5/- REWARD WILL BE GIVEN TO ANYONE GIVING SUCH INFORMATION AS WILL LEAD TO THE CONVICTION OF ANY PERSON FOUND DAMAGING OR REMOVING THIS APPARATUS OR USING IT FOR ANY OTHER PURPOSE THAN THAT FOR WHICH IT IS SUPPLIED.

Bath
Avon

Canals have always been a danger to the unwary, unskilled or foolhardy. Rewards for life-saving were offered, and even payments for fishing corpses from the waters. As these might vary from one parish to another, which bank you landed the body on could be a matter of financial significance.

Bath
Avon

The Kennet and Avon canal at
Sydney Gardens. It cost the promoters 2000 guineas to get leave
to construct the canal here, for
the gardens were a focus for a
lucrative housing development.
From 1801 to 1804 Jane Austen
lived in this desirable area.
When her father, the Rev.
George Austen, retired from his
parish in Hampshire, he took a
house at 4 Sydney Place.

Bath
Avon

In these more sophisticated
surroundings, wildlife is of a
different order – in this case,
ºa jaunty Mandarin duck.

Bath
Avon

A traditional building material, stone, combines successfully with the more modern use of pre-cast iron bridges. These examples, in Sydney Gardens, are dated 1800.

Bath
Avon

The spirit of a spa is still evident in Bath, through which the Kennet and Avon simply passed, with minimal business to transact in the town itself. The houses and gardens line the water as naturally as if it were a river, offering inspiration to the city fathers of industrial England for the enhancement of their environment.

Bath
Avon

The sudden increase in engine noise on going under the bridge in Sydney Gardens in Bath seems to trouble the crew.

Bath
Avon

In contrast to the basic practicality of most canal bridges, the Sydney Gardens bridge is ornamented in classical style.

Bath
Avon

The Kennet and Avon canal and the River Avon, together with the road and railway, squeeze through the narrow valley past steep fields and waterside gardens on the way to the east from Bath. The canal climbs away from the river until, at Claverton, the old water-powered pumping station lifts replenishing water 53 feet up from the Avon. The station opened in 1813 and may still be seen in operation today.

Claverton
Avon

Bridge abutments and other works in stone and brick are liable to damage, and in the days of horse-drawn boats special arrangements were taken to prevent injury from tow-ropes. As each tow-rope picked up grit from the path, it became abrasive and turned into an efficient cutting tool. The soft Bath stone was easily damaged. For protection, iron guard-plates were fixed where the tow-ropes rubbed against the bridge abutments. In other places these are iron or wooden rollers. It is a fascinating exercise to work out just how horse and boat were manoeuvred into locks and through bridges from the evidence of rope scars.

**Lympley Stoke
Avon**

A masterpiece by John Rennie, the Dundas aqueduct over the River Avon. This work, its near-by companion at Avoncliffe, and the aqueduct carrying the Lancaster Canal over the Lune are probably his finest structures. Built in local stone, it has suffered from the attacks of wind and rain. Indeed, Rennie was unhappy about using stone at all, advocating brick. His colleague, John Thomas, wrote in 1803, 'We still keep a sett of Masons repairing the Work which have been torn to pieces by the frost.'

**Lympley Stoke
Avon**

Stonework on the Dundas aqueduct shows signs of the weathering that disturbed its creator. The difficulty was that Bath stone needs to be 'seasoned', much like timber, before it is used. But the contractors who supplied materials to the canal builders were in too much haste to make their profit on the stone they had quarried.

**Loxwood
West Sussex**

The Wey and Arun canal was opened in 1818, just in time for its major objective to have disappeared. The scheme was to create an inland route, safe from the dangers of French warships, from London to Portsmouth. In 1811, when the matter was put in hand, and 1813, when an act was passed, the need appeared pressing, but the Battle of Waterloo changed everything. The work went ahead with dogged optimism, but the canal never carried sufficient trade to earn its keep, and it was abandoned in 1868. In some parts the route can still be seen. A ghostly derelict lock may be found in the woods.

**Alford
Surrey**

Isolated stretches of water now form ponds, but much of the canal's channel has been absorbed by farmland. In recent years initiatives to restore the Wey and Arun have come and gone, but a real prospect of its resurrection currently exists.

Little Venice
London

The Grand Union canal was completed to the Thames at Brentford in 1800, but boats had to make their way down the river to reach the city, a journey of 12 miles in tidal waters. The Paddington arm opened a year later and took boats from the junction at Bull's Bridge in Southall to a basin just east of today's railway station. In 1812 approval was given for the Regent's canal to carry the line around the north of the town and down to the Thames and the London Docks at Limehouse. The opening of this new route at its junction with the older canal half a mile north-west of its terminus created a new basin in the area now known as Little Venice. Here, the Grand Union is tree-lined and more evocative of Amsterdam than London.

Little Venice
London

Little Venice has developed a character all its own. The banks are lined with narrow boats, often moored two abreast, bringing colour and calm into the centre of London. The lives of houseboat dwellers overflow onto the banks, where container gardening gives rise to a business venture new to the waterways. The enhancement of Regent's Park by the canal was part of a planned landscape to beautify the city, but in Little Venice the benefit arises from personal initiatives.

Little Venice
London

The Paddington arm was built when this part of London was still open countryside. Urbanization followed swiftly, and the late-Georgian houses that face the canal, the speculative building of their time, now have the patina of age that excites admiration. Canal and town have matured together, and the crisp paintwork and polished brass of the boats provides a rich visual foil to the classic tree-lined residential quarter.

Little Venice
London

A passenger trip boat, properly equipped with life-belts as required by law, plies the Paddington arm. Packet boats for the carriage of passengers were a significant part of the business of the canals, both within urban areas and between towns. Public transport by road was by coach, cab or wagon – slow, uncomfortable and uncertain. By contrast, the packet boats were given priority on the canals and sped smoothly on their way, while the passengers enjoyed the space and opportunity to move about within the boat.

London

Traffic speeds along Westway, too busy to notice a Dutch sailing barge moored below on the Paddington arm. Of shallow draught and without a keel, these boats are fitted with lee boards that were lowered when required. The sailing barges of the Thames and Medway are somewhat similar but worked as coastal vessels in the main, extending their travels to the Thames but not to the canals.

Author's Acknowledgements

In the preparation of this work the author has drawn on the amazingly wide range of specialized and popular publications on the canals of England and Wales, but most valuable of all has been the enthusiasm and critical advice of Brian Collings of the Canal Museum at Stoke Bruerne. His patient assistance is most gratefully acknowledged.

The books most frequently referred to, and in some cases quoted from, were the following:

Clew, Kenneth R., *The Kennet & Avon Canal*, David & Charles, 1968
Dashwood, J. B., *The Thames to the Solent*, Longmans, Green, 1868 and Shepperton Swan, 1980
Defoe, Daniel, *A Tour through England and Wales*, 1724-26, and J. M. Dent (Everyman's Library), 1928
Hadfield, Charles, *British Canals*, David & Charles, 7th Ed., 1984
de Mare, Eric, *The Canals of England*, Alan Sutton, 1987
Owen, David, *Canals to Manchester*, Manchester University Press, 1977
Pratt, Frances, *Canal Architecture in Britain*, British Waterways Board, 1974
Rolt, L. T. C., *The Inland Waterways of England*, George Allen & Unwin, 2nd Ed., 1979
Rolt, L. T. C., *Landscape with Canals*, Allen Lane, 1977
Russell, Ronald (Ed), *Walking Canals*, David & Charles, 1984
Smiles, Samuel, *Lives of the Engineers*, John Murray, 1862
Squire, Roger W., *Canal Walks*, Hutchinson, 1985
Vine, P. A. L., *London's Lost Route to the Sea*, David & Charles, 4th Ed., 1986
Ware, Michael E., *Britain's Lost Waterways*, Moorland, 1989

Photographer's Notes

Photographing *Canals of England* presented me with a number of interesting challenges, not all technical. At times I found myself in search of landmarks described in texts written over two hundred years ago, and accessing locations Martin had taken pains to give directions to often meant long sojourns along the canals. However, it was rare to follow a tow-path for more than a couple of miles and not find an intriguing scene or feature, and my mountain bike became an essential partner in what were sometimes dawn to dusk escapades.

I used Fujichrome Velvia RVP for the majority of photographs and occasionally Fujichrome RDP 100D. I appreciate Velvia's strong saturated colour and find it works well not only in brilliant sunshine but even in very poor light conditions. The only filters used were skylight, polarizers and sometimes an 81A warming filter. Available light was used exclusively except for a portable strobe to illuminate the tree in the foreground of Pulteney Bridge, Bath.

Cameras were Nikon F4s with Nikon lenses from 20mm to 600mm and a Gitzo tripod. The 20mm lens was especially useful when water and sky were paramount or to emphasize the tunnel-like nature of some of the cuttings, also for creating graphic images. Nikon has superb optics and for awkward camera placements it was handy to be able to remove the viewfinder and look directly at the focusing screen. I often used the in-camera matrix and spot meters, particularly with polarizing filters. Additional incident metering was achieved with a Minolta Auto Meter III.

At times, the low amount of available light, my desire for broad depth of field and choice of slow film emulsions, resulted in long exposures, often many seconds and sometimes minutes. The look of water and leaves is particularly affected by long exposure times. Foam, bubbles and surface debris move with the current and the texture of water changes. Leaves moving in the breeze also blur, but I feel the compromise was worthwhile, preferring strong colours and finer grain, to the frozen motion faster film permits. When using long exposures, be sure to allow for reciprocity failure – many films require additional exposure beyond the metered reading.

To reduce vibration I used the camera's self-timer to release the shutter. For long exposures I set my Nikon F4's speed-dial to 'T' – the lens remaining open until the dial is advanced – and masked the lens with my hand before closing the shutter.

Technique is only part of the story, however, the cardinal rule of location photography is 'Be there!'. No amount of skill, laboratory retouching or computer manipulation can create the wonderful atmosphere and excitement of the sun as it breaks through black clouds on a dull day, perhaps only for seconds. Being there, and being prepared for the moment is what makes ordinary scenes extraordinary. I wasn't always able to make the sun shine, but I'm grateful for the opportunity provided by Michael Dover to have 'been there'. My thanks also to the people who use and work on the canals – a few of whom enliven this book – they ensure their preservation for the future.

Robert Reichenfeld

Information Offices, Museums and Associations

BRITISH WATERWAYS

NORTH-WEST REGION

Border Counties
Llangollen canal, Montgomery canal, Weaver navigation, Shropshire Union canal (Audlem to Ellesmere Port, including Middlewich branch)
Canal Office
Birch Road
Ellesmere, Shropshire SY12 9AA
Tel: 0691 622549

Leeds & Liverpool Canal, West, and Lancaster Waterway
Lancaster canal, Leeds & Liverpool canal (Greenbridge bridge 156 to Liverpool), St Helen's canal
Aldcliffe Road, Lancaster LA1 1SU
Tel: 0524 32712

Leeds & Liverpool Canal, East
Leeds & Liverpool canal (Greenbridge bridge 156 to Leeds)
Dobson Lock
Apperley Bridge
Bradford, West Yorkshire BD10 0PY
Tel: 0274 611303

Pennine and Potteries Waterways
Ashton, Caldon, Huddersfield, Macclesfield, Peak Forest, and Trent & Mersey (Preston Brook to Trentham) canals
Top Lock
Church Lane
Marple, Cheshire SK6 6BN
Tel: 061 427 1079

NORTH-EAST REGION

Aire and Calder Navigations
Aire and Calder navigation, Calder & Hebble navigation, Huddersfield Broad Canal
Lock Lane
Castleford

West Yorkshire WF10 2LH
Tel: 0977 554351

East Midlands and South Yorkshire
Chesterfield canal, Fossdyke and Witham navigations, Trent navigation (Gainsborough to Meadow Lane), Sheffield & South Yorkshire navigation, New Junction canal, Stainforth & Keadby canal
Mill Lane
Mill Gate
Newark
Nottinghamshire NG24 4TT
Tel: 0636 704481

Grand Union Canal, North
Erewash canal, Grand Union canal (West Bridge Leicester to Foxton, including Market Harborough arm), Grantham canal, Nottingham canal and Beeston cut, Soar navigation, Trent navigation (Derwent Mouth to Beeston Lock)
Trent Lock
Lock Lane
Long Eaton
Nottinghamshire NG10 2FF
Tel: 0602 461017

North Yorkshire Navigations
Ouse navigation, Pocklington canal, Ripon canal, Selby canal, Ure navigation
Naburn Lock
Naburn
North Yorkshire YO1 4RU
Tel: 0904 728229

MIDLANDS/SOUTH-WEST REGION

Gloucester
Gloucester & Sharpness canal and Gloucester Docks, Severn navigation
Llanthony Warehouse
Gloucester Docks
Gloucester GL1 2EJ
Tel: 0452 311192

Norbury
Shropshire Union canal (Audlem Bottom Lock to Autherley Junction), Stourbridge canal (Stourton to Wordsley aqueduct), Trent & Mersey canal (Trentham to Colwich Lock), Staffordshire & Worcestershire canal
Norbury Junction
Stafford, Staffordshire ST20 0PN
Tel: 0785 284253

Lapworth
Grand Union canal (Camp Hill Top Lock to Napton Junction), Stratford-Upon-Avon canal, Worcester & Birmingham canal
Brome Hall Lane
Lapworth
Solihull, West Midlands B94 5RB
Tel: 0564 784634

Govilon
Monmouthshire & Brecon canal, Swansea canal, Bridgewater & Taunton canal
The Wharf
Govilon
Abergavenny, Gwent NP7 9NY
Tel: 0873 830328

Bradley
Birmingham canal navigations, Birmingham & Fazeley canal (Farmers Bridge to Minworth Bottom Lock), Grand Union canal (Salford Junction to Camp Hill Top Lock), Stourbridge canal (Wordsley aqueduct to Black Delph)
Bradley Lane
Bilston, West Midlands WV14 8DW
Tel: 0902 409010

Fradley
Ashby canal, Birmingham & Fazeley canal (Minworth Bottom Lock to Whittington), Coventry canal, Trent & Mersey canal (Colwich Lock to Derwent Mouth)
Fradley Junction

Alrewas
Burton-on-Trent
Staffordshire DE13 7DN
Tel: 0283 790236

SOUTHERN REGION

Kennet & Avon Canal
River Avon (Bath to Hanham), Kennet & Avon canal
Bath Road
Devizes, Wiltshire SN10 1HB
Tel: 0380 722859

Oxford & Grand Union canal
Oxford canal (Oxford to Stone Bridge no. 9), Grand Union canal (Stowe Hill to Braunston and Norton Junction to Foxton, including Welford arm)
The Stop House
Braunston
Northamptonshire NN11 7JQ
Tel: 0788 890666

Grand Union Canal, South
Grand Union canal (Cowley to Stowe Hill, including Aylesbury, Northampton and Wendover arms)
Marsworth Junction
Watery Lane
Marsworth
Tring, Hertfordshire HP23 4LZ
Tel: 0442 825938

London and Lee & Stort
Grand Union canal (Brentford to Cowley, including Paddington and Slough arms), Hertford Union canal, Lee navigation, Regent's canal, Stort navigation, Bow Back rivers, Limehouse cut
The Toll House
Delamere Terrace
Little Venice, London W2 6ND
Tel: 071 286 6101

MUSEUMS

The Boat Museum
Dockyard Road
Ellesmere Port
South Wirral L65 4EF
Tel: 051 355 5017

Canal Exhibition
The Wharf
Llangollen
Clwyd, Wales
Tel: 0978 860702

Canal Museum
Canal Street
Nottingham
Tel: 0602 284602

Canal Museum
Stoke Bruerne
Towcester
Northamptonshire NN12 7SE
Te: 0604 862229

London Canal Museum
12/13 New Wharf Road
King's Cross
London N1 9RT
071 713 0836

National Waterways Museum
Llanthony Warehouse
Gloucester Docks
Gloucester GL1 2EH
Tel: 0452 307009

ASSOCIATIONS

The Inland Waterways Association
114 Regent's Park Road
London NW1 8UQ
071 586 2556

Inland Waterways Amenity Advisory Council
36 St Paul's Square
Birmingham B3 1QX
Tel: 021 212 1333

Index